PERFECT
FRENCH
COUNTRY

PERFECT
FRENCH COUNTRY

ROS BYAM SHAW

photography by

JAN BALDWIN

RYLAND PETERS & SMALL
LONDON • NEW YORK

Senior designer Toni Kay
Senior commissioning editor Annabel Morgan
Location research Jess Walton
Production manager Gordana Simakovic
Art director Leslie Harrington
Editorial director Julia Charles
Publisher Cindy Richards

First published in 2017 by
Ryland Peters & Small
20–21 Jockey's Fields,
London WC1R 4BW
and
341 East 116th Street
New York, NY 10029

www.rylandpeters.com

Text copyright © Ros Byam Shaw 2017
Design and photographs copyright
© Ryland Peters & Small 2017

10 9 8 7 6 5 4 3 2 1

ISBN 978-1-84975-799-7

A CIP record for this book is available
from the British Library.

Library of Congress CIP data has been applied for.

Printed and bound in China

For Richard

CONTENTS

INTRODUCTION

Owners of two of the houses on the following pages describe them as 'paradise'. Michel Mulder telephoned his wife-to-be, Sofie Sleumer, after first viewing the cluster of cottages they have made their home, and said 'I have found paradise'. He hasn't changed his mind. Thekla Benevello talks of the 15th-century *manoir* where she lives in a converted 18th-century barn, as 'my paradise on earth'. Maybe more owners would have said the same, had I asked the right question. But two out of thirteen is nonetheless striking. It doesn't get better than paradise.

From the point of view of a medieval peasant, a 19th-century mill worker, or even a Roman emperor, many of us in the developed world live in paradise. We have anaesthetics, antibiotics, and enough to eat. We can fly to the other side of the world in hours, communicate instantly, record every moment. We have entertainment in our hands, and knowledge at our fingertips.

We have adjusted to all these advances so quickly that we take them for granted. They provide the conditions that make earthly paradise possible, but they are not the active ingredients. The essential attributes that make Michel and Thekla feel they live in heaven are not the quality of the plumbing or the magic of electricity. They are much older, deeper things: the sound of birdsong, the beauty of trees, the curve of the river, the sense of space, a freshly laid egg for breakfast; and the way the buildings that shelter them relate to the landscape, and speak of the generations who used and inhabited them long before the texts, tweets, additives, and packaging of the 21st century.

In a world that can seem overcrowded, the French countryside still feels big, gloriously empty, and refreshingly untamed. There are deer and wild boar in the forests, there are roads through fields of wheat and barley in the north, sunflowers and lavender in the south, where you can drive all day and only meet a few other cars. There are quiet villages where nothing seems to have changed since the invention of tarmac, and there are

markets where people sell fruit picked from their orchards the day before, vegetables dusted with the earth they grew in, cheese made in small local dairies, and wine from vineyards down the road.

One of the great pleasures of writing this book was the lunches provided by hospitable owners who insisted we interrupted our work and sat down, if only for 20 minutes, in order to eat. Without exception these were simple but memorable meals, eaten outdoors under a tree or a vine-draped pergola. Views ranged from the ravishing distant peaks of the Pyrenees, to the rippling reflections of woodland in a millpond.

No one does a lunch of cheese and bread better than the French. But this is not a book about food; it is a book about interiors, and how people arrange and decorate them. Here again, the French excel. Ever since the 17th and 18th centuries, when France led the way in all things fashionable including interior design, the French have displayed an enviable degree of domestic chic. When it comes to creating rooms that are both relaxed and elegant, French country house style is hard to beat. Fortunately, it is not impossible to emulate or borrow from, even if your own slice of paradise is on a different continent.

GRADUAL CONVERSION

*E*very three to four weeks, Fiona Atkins drives from her home in Islington through *South London and across Kent, to the Eurotunnel crossing at Folkestone. When she emerges in France she drives another four hours through Normandy, past Caen, until she comes to a small, quiet village with two streets of old houses built in stone the colour of set honey, and a sturdy church under a steep roof of dark brown clay tiles. Usually she is on her own. Her husband, Clifford, is a lawyer, and has limited time to spare. So, although the house fills up on high days and holidays, and their two grown-up daughters come when they can, Fiona is the most regular, consistent visitor.*

PREVIOUS PAGES The buildings of this former farm date from three periods: a 19th-century barn (not seen in this picture) that borders the village street, the 18th-century, double-fronted farmhouse, and a 17th-century single-storey building that once housed both the farmer and his animals.

ABOVE On the other side of the 17th-century building is a swimming pool and a dining terrace, which can be closed off from the courtyard with the ornate wrought-iron gates. The door at the top of the steps leads to a barn where there is an antique cider press that Clifford intends to restore.

OPPOSITE ABOVE LEFT TO RIGHT An antique bench and a vintage folding chair outside the entrance to the newest of the buildings, a 19th-century barn that has been converted to make guest accommodation. The original farm building is draped with climbing roses. On a wall of the passage that once separated the farmer and his family from the animals, a wooden hen coop holds pots of geraniums.

OPPOSITE BELOW The roof space above the single-storey farm building would originally have been used as a hayloft, accessed from outside through this gabled opening. The small, oval window is a charming architectural feature typical of old farm buildings in this region of France.

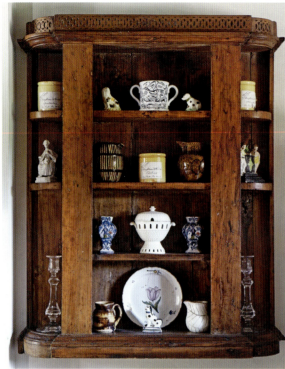

ABOVE To the right of the kitchen chimney breast, shelves display a mix of 18th- and early-19th-century pottery.

RIGHT When Fiona and Clifford bought the house, the room that is now the kitchen had been divided to make a small downstairs bathroom and a corridor. They removed the partition walls and installed a new floor. At the centre of the room is a round table made from a painted metal clock face, perhaps from a town hall or a church.

In London, Fiona's working life has several strands. In 2002 she bought a derelict early-18th-century terraced house on Fournier Street, opposite the soaring white Portland stone of Hawksmoor's Christ Church, Spitalfields. The house had no plumbing and only rudimentary electric lighting, but its original features, including panelling and staircase, were intact. With the help of architect Jeremy Amos, Fiona restored the house and opened an antiques shop in the ground-floor rooms. More recently, she expanded the shop into the basement, where she started serving tea, coffee, and cake. At the same time, she converted a small building in the back garden into a gallery, selling mainly British 20th-century art.

This space is the venue for occasional shows by contemporary artists as well as an annual exhibition curated by Fiona. The beautifully furnished and decorated rooms above the shop are available to rent as self-catering holiday accommodation. And, as if all that were not enough, Fiona also organizes talks and workshops on subjects as various as decorating ceramics and the history of scent.

You might wonder why someone with so much already on her plate would choose to pile it even higher with a third property in a foreign country, with another garden to cultivate, a swimming pool to clean, and the endless routine maintenance that accompanies any house, particularly an old one. Fiona sees it differently. 'As soon as I am through the tunnel and in France, the tension seems to slip off my shoulders,' she says. 'This house is a retreat – somewhere I come to get away, to think, to write, to recharge. I always look forward to coming, and return feeling rested.'

Fiona and Clifford acquired the house almost by default. 'We used to come here for holidays when our girls were young, and it is an area we grew to love. We drove past this house for sale and got very excited by the idea of buying it. It was a wreck, and Clifford's parents offered to take it on, with the idea that we

could all use it. The first thing they did was to hire an English builder, who turned out to be a complete disaster. He camped on site and spent all the money they paid him on wine.'

At this point, Fiona and Clifford stepped in. Fiona took charge – 'Clifford was far too busy being a lawyer, and he trusts me.' Fiona found French builders, recommended by a friend. 'They were brilliant, and rather more reliable than their predecessor.' The 'wreck' they had decided to rescue consisted of a 19th-century barn on the village street, an 18th-century farmhouse set at right angles below it down a slope, and on the far side of this house, a little lower still and running more or less parallel with the newer barn, a building that dates from the 16th or early 17th century and is the original farmhouse. Long and low, with a roof as deep as the walls are high, this earliest piece of the architectural melange is bisected by a wide, arched passageway. One end was living accommodation, while the other housed animals. The attic space above in the high pitch of the roof was for storing hay and fodder.

OPPOSITE Fiona's study, where she works at a 19th-century, painted Italian desk, watched by a small, stuffed crocodile, is on the other side of the staircase from the kitchen. The painting above the desk is an unsigned, 19th-century French naive painting of buildings in a landscape. Like the kitchen floor, the floor in this room is made from squares of terracotta tiles enclosed by bands of oak.

ABOVE AND LEFT Opposite the desk, a pair of early-20th-century leather armchairs flank the fireplace, above which hangs a painting by British artist Ann Tooth who mainly exhibited in the 1930s. Next to the antique dividers on the mantelpiece is a French weathervane. The marble sculpture on the sideboard is by a contemporary French artist, Sylvie Plu, and dates from the 1990s.

'This house is a retreat – somewhere I come to get away, to think, to write, to recharge. I always look forward to coming, and return feeling rested.'

Today all these buildings have been colonized, but 20 years ago the barns were unsafe, with holes in the floors and crumbling stonework, and the priority was to make the house between them habitable. This retained its old layout of two rooms on the ground and first floors, and another two in the attic. A corridor ran along the back of the house downstairs, and a very small bathroom had been inserted in a corner of the kitchen. Leading off the kitchen was a single-storey *fromagerie*. Over the years since work on the buildings began, the space has been completely reorganized. The main house was finished in 2002, in tandem with the house on Fournier Street, and with the help of the same architect. The *fromagerie* is now a sitting room, and the room on the opposite side of the stairs from the kitchen is Fiona's study. Upstairs, a bit of re-jigging created two bedrooms and two bathrooms, with a third bedroom and shower-room in the attic over the *fromagerie*, and two more bedrooms in the attic of the farmhouse.

In the kitchen and study, they laid floors of reclaimed terracotta *tomettes* combined with oak. Fiona found antique fireplaces for the study and sitting room, and windows and shutters were repaired. In 2006 they tackled the top barn, creating a big, bright living space, with a guest bedroom upstairs. In 2007 it was the swimming pool. Then came the terracing of the ground between the buildings, and the creation of a courtyard surrounded by flower beds. Finally, they annexed the domestic end of the early farmhouse by knocking a door

ABOVE Double doors made in oak open from the living room onto three steps that lead down into the older farmhouse, a space that has now been converted into a games room. Doors, panelling, and staircase were designed by architect Jeremy Amos, and the metal stair balusters and handrail were made by a local French blacksmith. The stairs lead up to two guest bedrooms and a bathroom.

OPPOSITE In a corner of the games room, a pair of Art Deco chairs flanks an early-20th-century double seat from a children's fairground ride. The knobbly cushions are from 7 Upholstery in Shoreditch, and the resin lamp base is from Marianna Kennedy, Fiona's neighbour in Spitalfields. The notch in the walls marks the original ceiling height.

LEFT An extra bedroom was created in the roof space above the old *fromagerie*, now the living room. Against the back wall, Fiona has used metal grilles from an early-20th-century French lift cage lined with gathered fabric to make cupboard doors.

BELOW The main bedroom, above the study, has a charming architectural flourish of engaged pilasters above an original marble chimney piece. The painting is unsigned, early 20th century. Fiona bought it in England, but thinks it might be French.

OPPOSITE On the far side of the *lit bateau* stands a French mirror dating from the second half of the 19th century. The chair, upholstered in sky blue, is an 18th-century French *duchesse brisée* that would once have had a matching footstool allowing for elegant lounging. There is no need for curtains/drapes, as there are outside shutters.

'My aim has always been to sell affordable, decorative, attractive things for people's homes,' Fiona says. Her own house is an excellent advertisement.

through from the sitting room. Its ground floor is now a big games room, from the middle of which a simple, oak staircase leads up to two bedrooms and a bathroom.

Furnishing the house, like its layout and design, has been Fiona's responsibility. As the daughter of antiques dealer John Jackson, whose Brighton shop was a well-known source of fine English furniture, paintings, and Chinese *objets*, Fiona says she tried hard not to follow in his footsteps, studying Classics at Oxford and then working on logistics for a company that laid submarine cabling. She succumbed after having children, and opened a shop on Columbia Road. This house is full of her finds, some conventionally lovely like the 18th-century painted sofa in the sitting room, some more unusual like the huge metal clock face for which she commissioned a base to make a kitchen table. On the walls hang a selection of charming paintings. It's the same mix as in her shop. 'My aim has always been to sell affordable, decorative, attractive things,' she says. Her own house is an excellent advertisement.

MEMORIES OF CHILDHOOD

*T*he small, painted sign is misleading. Tucked into a hedge at the side of a lane, it points along a woodland track and reads 'Le Grand Moulin'. If you take the turning, down through the dappled canopy of leaves, you will find yourself in a grassy clearing beside a large pond. Set back from its edge are three modest buildings, one with a dormer window set into its roof, one a single-storey barn camouflaged by a thick mantle of creeper, the third a rustic confection with a weathered timber frame, a ladder staircase, metal windows, and a roof of corrugated iron – more den than house. No sign of anything that might be described as 'grand', no heavy wheel driving giant cogs, just the reflection of trees in still water, and a plume of wood smoke rising from a chimney.

PREVIOUS PAGES An early morning mist floats across the surface of the millpond. Françoise has furnished the jetty with a table and chairs, and guests in the cabin often dine here on warm summer evenings, when the only sounds are birdsong, the occasional buzzing of a stag beetle, and the rush of water that cascades from the pond through a pipe next to the old mill.

ABOVE The mill house is the largest of the three buildings in the clearing. The single-storey extension once housed the machinery for the mill, which ground flour.

OPPOSITE ABOVE LEFT TO RIGHT Dotted around the edge of the pond are picturesque antiques hardy enough to live outdoors, such as these birdcages. The door to the converted barn where Françoise lives is painted a traditional Normandy red. The cabin, with its corrugated iron roof, was originally built as a log store.

OPPOSITE BELOW The painted wooden door into the mill opens directly into the single room that once housed the miller and his family.

BELOW At right angles to the mill is a single-storey barn that Françoise has converted to make a house for herself. The space is divided into three rooms. The front door opens into this kitchen and living room, beyond which is a bathroom and a passage that leads to the bedroom at the far end. The refrigerator is clad in metal.

RIGHT Françoise used old window frames to make the sliding doors of this cupboard on the wall opposite the sink where she stores all her crockery and glass, much of which is antique. Despite the extreme rusticity of her surroundings, Françoise entertains in style, lighting the candles in her chandelier, and serving wine in 18th-century glasses.

OPPOSITE Françoise designed the dining table, which has a top made from the slate top of an old billiard table, and also the seating – metal stools that push underneath the table when not in use, and a banquette padded with cushions that doubles as her sofa. The house is heated by a wood-burning stove. The remains of a traditional Normandy *bourdin aux pommes* is on the table after lunch eaten outside under the shade of a huge lime tree.

Dotted around this waterside hamlet are tables and garden chairs in curly painted metal, topiary balls, and elegant urns planted with box, poppies, or geraniums. There is a jetty jutting into the pond, where a table is draped with a cloth and adorned with a rusty candelabra. Beneath a huge lime tree, a wooden trestle holds zinc jugs, stone bottles, a metal sculpture of a chicken, and an agricultural rake. Everywhere you look there is a charming vignette, a place to sit or lounge, a view to be enjoyed. The only sound is birdsong and the rush of water that tumbles from the pond through a pipe and into the stream below.

Presiding over this bucolic playground is its owner and creator, Françoise Piccino, whose rosy cheeks and curls make her look far too girlish to be grandmother to a 26-year-old. Since Françoise is not as young as she looks,

OPPOSITE Françoise's bedroom was once the smokehouse and retains its original fireplace, which was used for smoking hams. Françoise has made a canopy for her bed with antique hemp and linen sheets that have been dyed a soft terracotta. Her bedspread is in the same fabric. Opposite the foot of the bed, a table holds a collection of treasured antiques, including a metal-studded, 18th-century leather travelling trunk.

this seems an unlikely place to choose to live at a stage in life when most people seek convenience and the safety net of a surrounding community. But she is a romantic. 'This land has been in my family for four generations,' she says. 'I grew up nearby, and we used to come here on a Sunday for picnics and to fish in the pond. No one had lived here for years, but as a little girl I used to dream of moving here one day.' Ten years ago, Françoise decided to do just that.

The biggest of the buildings, the stone house with the dormer window, is the original mill, and was probably used for flour. It has a single living room, an attic above, and a larger room next door where the machinery was housed. Françoise's father put a new roof on, adding the dormer window to make a habitable upstairs space. The smaller, single-storey building, set at a right-angle to the mill, was a barn, and attached to it was a timber-framed wood store. Françoise restored the barn first, putting in a new floor, installing a wood-burning stove, and making a bedroom at one end, a kitchen and living room at the other, and a bathroom in between, and this is where she lives.

ABOVE LEFT In the passage that links the kitchen and living room with the bedroom, metal shelves hold a couple of favourite framed landscapes. Both the door to the bedroom and to the bathroom are reclaimed, the bathroom given privacy by means of an antique linen hand towel draped over the glass. The floor throughout the barn is reclaimed, hexagonal *tomettes*.

ABOVE RIGHT The side of the bathtub is clad in reclaimed planks and towels are stored in wire shelving. By a careful editing of her possessions, Françoise has given the three rooms of her small, secluded home a sense of commodious luxury.

The timber frame of the wood store was detached from the end of the barn and shunted a few metres away, then converted to make a cabin with the addition of reclaimed windows and doors. Named *La Cabane de Jeanne* (Françoise's full name is Françoise-Marie-Jeanne), it contains a double bed with pristine, lace-trimmed bedlinen, a tiny shower, and a miniature kitchen on the ground floor, and a big seating and dining area above.

The *cabane* is understandably popular and, more often than not, Françoise has company in her woodland idyll. She also has frequent visits from customers who appreciate her taste for 18th- and 19th-century French furnishings. Aged 30, she started dealing in antiques, turning a hobby into a career, and until two years ago she ran a shop. Her remaining stock is now stored in the machine room of the old mill and is steadily disappearing into the cars of friends and clients who still buy from her. When it has all gone, she will move from the barn into this building. 'I have always lived in big houses,' she says. 'When my husband was alive, we restored three houses, the last one another old mill, in Lot-et-Garonne. It will be good to have room for my piano and sofas.'

Meanwhile, she has made brilliant use of the limited space in the barn. Her combined kitchen, dining, and

RIGHT Françoise says there would always have been a bed in the corner of this ground-floor room in the mill house, as this is where the miller and his family cooked, ate, and slept. All the furnishings are antique French country pieces, though perhaps a little more grand than a humble miller could have afforded.

living room feels bigger than its footprint, partly thanks to the ceiling that extends up into the beamed pitch of the roof, partly because of the way Françoise has used mirrors to give the illusion of extra volume, and partly because the table with its surrounding cushioned seating fits so neatly, having been designed and commissioned by Françoise to fill the available space. There are no doors between the kitchen and the lobby alongside the bathroom, and this also serves to expand the room.

The bedroom was once a smokehouse and retains its hefty stone fireplace and raised grate. Here Françoise has made a bed canopy by attaching antique linen sheets, dyed a soft shade of terracotta, to the wooden beams of the old ceiling. Just as the kitchen is also the dining room and the sitting room, the bedroom doubles as a study. Françoise's laptop looks exotically modern on a table against the wall, and the WiFi connection seems almost magical in this old-fashioned rural setting.

Although the mill has no kitchen or bathroom as yet, Françoise has furnished its original living room and can sometimes be found sitting in an armchair next to a blaze of logs in its capacious stone fireplace. The miller and his family occupied this one room and there is still a bed in the corner next to the fireplace where it would always have been. The bed canopy is patterned, with raised embroidery, a chequered border, and a bobble fringe. It might have hung here for a hundred years, its faded pink picking up the traditional Normandy rusty red of the beamed ceiling and the rosy brown of the clay floor tiles, but Françoise put it up and says it is a skirt made for an African tribal chief. On a side table are three pairs of children's wooden and leather clogs, or *sabots*. Françoise picks up the black pair. 'Unlike the bed canopy, these have been here for a long time,' she says. 'They belonged to my great-great-grandmother, and I found them in the alcove next to the fire.'

ABOVE Just to the right of the front door into the mill house, a door covered by a curtain leads into the room that used to house the mill machinery. Françoise plans to convert this large space into a living room where she can have her piano and sofas. On the table are three pairs of children's *sabots*. Françoise found the pair on the right in a niche next to the chimney breast. They belonged to her great-great-grandmother.

OPPOSITE The canopy of the bed, with its pom-pom fringe and appliquéd ribbon embroidery, looks as though it could be 18th century but was actually made by Françoise from the wrap-around skirt of an African tribal chieftan. The large red cushion on top of the bed is an old French quilt, filled with down, surprisingly light and extremely warm.

ABOVE The *cabane*, or cabin, was originally built by Françoise's father as a log store, and was attached to one end of the barn where she now lives. Françoise had it dismantled and moved, to create space between it and the barn, and then made it habitable using reclaimed windows and doors to enclose a bedroom, bathroom, and tiny kitchen on the ground floor.

LEFT Upstairs in the *cabane,* a living and dining space is tucked beneath the corrugated iron roof. Partially open to the elements, it has the slightly makeshift feel of a grown-up den. There is a view through the reclaimed metal windows across the pond and to the woodland beyond.

OPPOSITE The space is simply furnished with a table with padded seating behind it, and a padded ottoman bench on the other side. The vintage coffee set is 'Scraffito' by Habitat, and magazines are stored in a metal shop rack, painted bright red.

'I grew up nearby, and we used to come here on a Sunday for picnics and to fish in the pond. No one had lived here for years, but as a little girl I used to dream of moving here one day.'

PEAK VIEWING

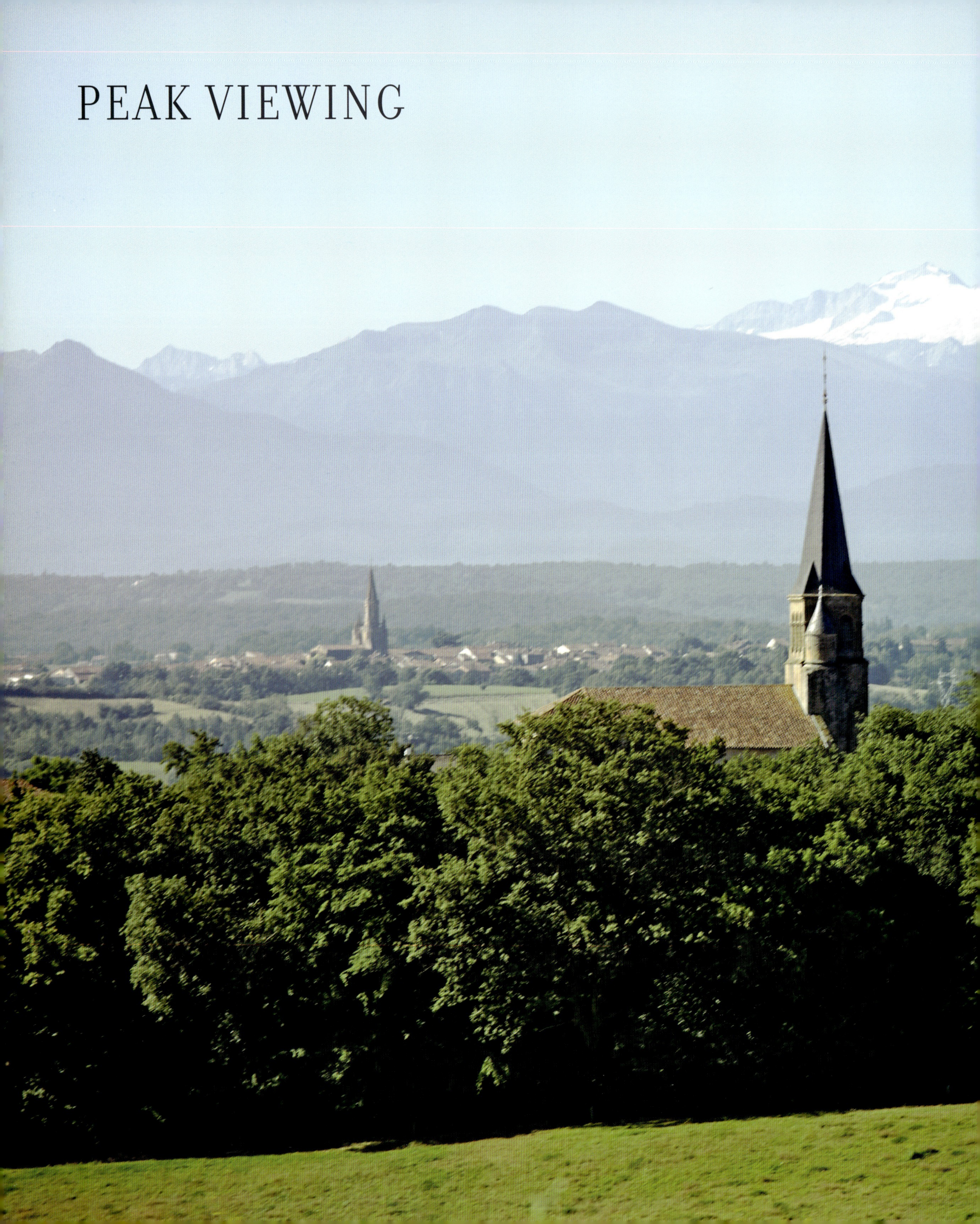

'I have a crush on France,' says Ilse van de Meerakker. 'I married a French man and I came to live here, and stayed for 12 years.' The marriage didn't work out and Ilse went back to The Netherlands, where she established a successful business running a shop and a website selling furnishings, as well as taking on commissions as an interior decorator. But she missed France and decided to look for a holiday home. 'It took four years of searching,' she says. 'I wanted to find somewhere with no "buts" – somewhere that had no disadvantages. I was staying not far from here, and I asked in the village if anyone knew of something nice for sale. This house had just come on the market, and the minute I saw it, I wanted to buy it. After all, who could resist that incredible view?'

PREVIOUS PAGES The spectacular view past the church spire of the nearest village, across the spire of the next village, and towards the jagged line of the Pyrenees spreads in front of the house like a giant picture postcard. The house is located down a long track that leads off a country road, and the only sounds are birdsong and the chime of church bells.

ABOVE LEFT AND RIGHT By infilling a side of the open barn that extends from one end of the L-shaped building, Ilse and Joseph have created a shady dining terrace that takes full advantage of the view, furnishing it with a table big enough to seat their extended family, whether for breakfast or dinner. After dark, the space is illuminated by the candles in glass lanterns on the bamboo console table.

OPPOSITE Double doors from the terrace lead into the seating area of the open-plan living room. Here an expanse of plasterboard wall, built out against the original stone walls of the barn, hides all the wiring, and provides a shelf for the display of some of Ilse's collection of pots and vases.

The view is certainly a good one, and the house takes full advantage of it. Set by a farm track that curves through fields, the house presents a blank, almost windowless face as you approach. But drive through the gate and come round its other side and the beauty of its location is apparent. Here, in front of the building, the land slides from the short grass of lawn across the gravel drive and into the taller grass and wild flowers of fields, with not even a fence to separate them. Every window, and the covered terrace, shares the same magnificent vista – a carpet of countryside, etched by the darker mounds and pillars of hedges and trees, rolling away to a hazy distance where the shadow-shapes of the Pyrenees run along the horizon under a broad band of white cloud. Piercing the middle of this broad, green landscape, the church steeple in a nearby village is clear and sharp as a needle.

The house was originally a farm. Ilse points out the new farmhouse where the farmer who once lived here has relocated, a pink house, just visible to the left of the steeple. The farmer had already gone when Ilse bought the property, and the process of conversion from working farm to holiday home had already begun. The new owners had got as far as converting the original stone farmhouse of two rooms downstairs and two rooms above, which they had stripped back and opened up to create a single living room on the ground floor, and a bedroom and bathroom reached up a metal spiral staircase. The roof beams had been replaced, as had the floorboards, and the rough stone walls had been re-plastered, leaving just a few stones bare for rustic effect.

RIGHT The original structure of these 18th- and 19th-century farm buildings has been left bare, the old stone and timbers exposed. In sharp contrast with the antique shell of the building, pristine white plasterboard forms a long, deep shelf along the back wall, again hiding wiring and providing display space. A steep wooden staircase leads up to two bedrooms, also encased in white plasterboard.

Attached to this relatively small, now two-room house was a large barn for which Ilse had grand plans. She waited for a year before putting them into practice, giving herself time to think through exactly how she wanted to use this space. By this stage, Ilse had a new partner, Joseph van Capel, a hairdresser who owns a salon in the Dutch town where Ilse also lives. In 2014, they hired a team of three builders from Holland, and work began. Between them, Ilse and Joseph have six children, so a priority was to make more bedroom space. This they achieved by inserting a mezzanine floor above the area of the barn that has become the kitchen and utility room. These platforms under the pitch of the old oak beams have waist-height walls that give the two bedroom spaces some privacy, while also affording a bird's-eye view over the room below.

THIS PAGE AND OPPOSITE The dining table was made on site, using offcuts of wood. On the low shelf behind is a still life of pottery, metalwork, baskets, and pictures. The window above the table retains its original shutter.

LEFT Large blocks of stone mark the position of the wall that once divided the barns from the old farmhouse, now knocked through to make a single building. The bedrooms above the kitchen area have waist-height walls, allowing an uninterrupted view of the old roof timbers, and of the dining table below. The kitchen area is to the left.

OPPOSITE ABOVE The main bedroom and bathroom occupy the whole of the first floor of the old farmhouse. Part of the timber stud wall with its infill of cob, which once divided this space into smaller rooms, has been retained to act as a partition between the bedroom and bathroom. The post of the metal spiral staircase can be seen between the timber studs to the right.

OPPOSITE BELOW LEFT Both the bed and the bath are positioned to enjoy the view of distant mountains. The bed sits opposite one window, and the bath directly in front of the other one. Curtains are squares of heavy, cotton canvas, and have eyelets at their top corners so that they can be hooked into place.

OPPOSITE BELOW RIGHT Ilse bought the ornate armoire locally. She painted it dark grey and uses it to to store towels and bedlinen.

The Dutch builders stayed for three weeks. Ilse and Joseph left them to get on with the work: the insulation and planking of the roof, the plumbing, and electricity. Their final task was to lay a poured-concrete floor that would flow throughout the L-shaped space, uniting kitchen, dining, and sitting areas in a seamless sheet of pale, polished grey. When Ilse arrived with her teenage son at the end of the three weeks, having driven all night, and hoping to see the shell of their new home complete and ready for painting and the installation of the kitchen units, she was horrified to discover that, far from smooth and seamless, the poured concrete had the texture of gravel. 'The concrete mixer truck had got lost and taken much longer to arrive than it should have done, and the mixture had dried out in the heat,' she explains. 'My son and I had to add another layer on top. It was exhausting, but this time it worked.'

All the finishing, the painting, and the tiling was done by Ilse and Joseph. Any work that has not been completed is waiting for an outside contractor; the rail for the spiral staircase, for example, which has been on order for three years. Meanwhile,

Ilse has furnished the converted barn with favourite items of stock from her shop, which she closed over a year ago. There are also things, such as the long pine dining table, that they made themselves on site, or bought locally and restored, in the case of the old wooden armoire in the bedroom that Ilse painted in a smart, dark grey. Crisp, modern pieces such as the Eames-style dining chairs with their pristine white plastic seats, and the square-edged sofa covered in white canvas, make a pleasing contrast with the rough golden stone of the old walls, and the heavily textured grain of the rafters.

At the far end of the L-shape, round the corner from the kitchen, French doors stand open onto a large terrace, created in an open-sided barn with a roof that provides welcome shade for outside dining. At the other end of the house, but not attached to it, is another barn, a simple metal framework with a shallow, pitched roof. When they have cleared it of building materials, they think they might use it as an outdoor games room. 'I can't wait until there is nothing more to do,' says Ilse. 'What I would really like is to come here for long enough to get bored.'

AFTER A
FASHION

*I*rene Silvagni has legendary status in the world of fashion. Over a long career, which began when she was asked by a friend of her husband to become Paris correspondent for an Italian magazine, and which progressed through jobs as fashion editors on French Elle, American Vogue, and French Vogue, and culminated in becoming European envoy for designer Yohji Yamamoto, she gained a reputation as a style maverick, with an eye for innovation, a disregard for convention, and a genius for spotting new talent. One of those rare women who exude style without making any apparent effort, she is more hippy than fashionista, more gypsy than couture.

PREVIOUS PAGES The house is a small, Renaissance mansion, one room deep. This, its front facade, faces north, and is protected from the summer sun by mature trees, including a fig and a plane tree. Under the shelter of their canopies, Irene has placed chairs, tables, and metal beds for daytime lounging.

OPPOSITE ABOVE LEFT TO RIGHT Plant stands support rows of pots containing spiky aloe vera. The outdoor shutters at the front of the house are painted a gentle shade of green. A door into one of the barns on the far side of the rear courtyard.

OPPOSITE BELOW LEFT TO RIGHT The kitchen window looks out onto one of several tables in the courtyard, all of which are placed to make the most of shade at different times of day. Early on a summer's day, the morning glory clambering up the wall is at its most beautiful. Shade is essential in this climate and next to the pool is provided by a wooden pergola draped with wisteria.

ABOVE At the back, the house faces south onto a courtyard enclosed by two smaller wings. A central tree provides shade and the space is scattered with chairs and tables as well as being home to a host of pot plants, including many succulents.

In 1989, two years after she joined French *Vogue*, Irene and her husband, Italian film producer and designer Giorgio Silvagni, were staying in Provence when Giorgio saw an advertisement in the window of an estate agent that read *Ruine à Vendre*. It intrigued him and he persuaded Irene to come with him to see it the next day. More than a quarter of a century later, it is Irene's permanent home. Sitting at the kitchen table, still glamorous in her mid-seventies, she tells the story of finding it as if it is as fresh in her mind as yesterday.

'Oh yes, it was a ruin,' she says. 'But something happened when we entered these abandoned rooms, something very difficult to explain. We both felt it. That this was where we should drop our luggage, this was where we should settle.' At the time they were living in Paris. But they bought the ruin that had spoken to them, and started spending time here on the edge of the Camargue, where orchards are decked with the pink globes of peaches and nectarines, figs grow fat and purple, and the summer is hot, long, and loud with the crackle of cicadas.

LEFT AND ABOVE The front door in the north facade opens onto a simple, stone staircase. Giorgio limewashed the walls himself, using lines of colour to emphasize architectural features such as doorways. The rooms are *en enfilade*, leading one into the other so you can see along the whole length of the house through their doorways. Here (left), standing in the second staircase hall, created by Irene and Giorgio, with the kitchen behind you, you can see through the Moroccan library, the Turkish dining room, and the original entrance hall into the red salon at the far end of the house.

OPPOSITE In the red salon, Giorgio paved the floor with pebbles, a traditional type of flooring in Provençal houses. An antique metal bed is presided over by huge pottery jars.

OVERLEAF The kitchen is at the opposite end of the house from the red salon and was created in a space that once housed animals. Giorgio painted the walls in strong bands of colour, and designed the central unit with its brushed-steel top and metal shelving. The floor is polished concrete and the back door leads into the courtyard.

OPPOSITE AND ABOVE A long sideboard in the kitchen holds pottery dishes of fruit and vegetables. The elegant wrought-iron wall braces, bought in a flea market, now have a purely decorative function, and hang above Indian metal wall plaques depicting Ganesh playing a series of musical instruments. On the far side of the kitchen, part of the wall is clad in stainless-steel sheets, and colourful French pottery is stacked on a metal table.

RIGHT Dry foods are stored in armoires in the pantry next to the kitchen, where a metal table holds eggs, new potatoes, and a dish of glossy aubergines/eggplants.

The house dates from the second half of the 17th century and was built as a summer retreat by an aristocrat from Avignon. It sits in farmland, screened by hedges and trees, in an oasis of garden, its north-facing facade protected by a mature fig and a tall plane tree, and draped in a thick padding of creeper. Doors stand open, shutters ajar. If you enter the house through French doors at one end, you will find yourself in a deep red cocoon of a living room, with a cobbled floor. If you walk to the other end, through an *enfilade* of the butter-yellow staircase hall, the terracotta 'Turkish' dining room, the 'Moroccan' library, and the second staircase hall, you come to the kitchen, from where a door leads into an enclosed courtyard the size of a tennis court on the other side of the house, furnished with tables and chairs, metal plant stands, and terracotta pots.

When they bought the house there was no electricity and no plumbing. 'We had to dig for water,' says Irene. They also had to raise the floor level, as the house had been prone to flooding. Giorgio tiled the floor of the red salon with pebbles, as is traditional in this area of France. As is also traditional, one end of the house had been used for animals. This is the space they made the kitchen, creating a fourth bedroom and bathroom in the hayloft above. As the upstairs rooms were also *en enfilade*, they built a second staircase so that the middle bedrooms can be accessed individually.

Ten years ago Giorgio Silvagni died. 'I lost him,' says Irene, patting her heart, 'but he is still here, still with me.' His presence is certainly strong in this house, into which he put so much time and creativity. And not just his face, looking out

'We both brought
our own tastes,
and our own
backgrounds and
cultures into this
house,' says Irene.

BELOW In the original staircase hall, a pair of 20th-century modernist chairs stands against mottled yellow limewashed walls, and next to an old cast iron radiator. The heavy curtain pulls across the front door to keep out winter draughts.

RIGHT AND OPPOSITE This room is known as the 'Turkish' dining room, in honour of the suzanis that drape two of the sofas. The demi-lune console table was made by Giorgio from the railings of a wrought-iron balcony, and the wall light above, also made by him, is mounted on a 17th-century carved wooden banister. The chandelier is hung with two original 'revolutionary' lanterns that were carried on long poles. The others were made in India to match them.

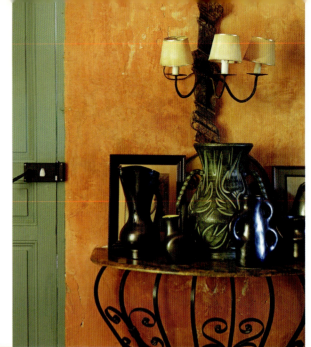

from some of the chic black-and-white photographs by favourite fashion photographers, many of whose careers Irene launched. His hurried brush strokes pattern the walls in vibrant shades of limewash – cobalt blue in one bedroom, soft mint green in another, clotted cream on a landing. In the green bedroom he added a delicate frieze of leaves, in the kitchen horizontal stripes of French grey and brick red. There is also furniture designed and made by him with the help of local artisans, as well as pieces he put together from bits of architectural salvage, such as the pair of consoles in the dining room with metal bases that began life as balconies, and the wall lights above them, mounted on fragments of antique wooden balustrade.

Irene's contributions to the interior include the antique and second-hand fabrics, from silk damasks and glazed chintzes, to Indian embroideries, which hang as curtains or on the walls, serve as tablecloths and bedspreads, cover cushions and screens, and are draped thickly over chairs and sofas. She loves textiles and, although she usually wears black, the walk-in wardrobe/closet in her bedroom is a rainbow of ethnic pattern. 'We both brought our own tastes, and our own backgrounds and cultures into this house,' explains Irene.

OPPOSITE The blue bedroom is above the red salon and accessed by the original staircase. The clay floor tiles are original, and have a beautiful, polished patina, while also being very broken. Giorgio made the simple, planked headboard, which he also painted blue, and that supports an 18th-century painting of the Madonna from a church.

ABOVE The blue bedroom has its own bathroom, in a part of the room sectioned off by screens, but leading off the landing next to it is this separate bathroom, painted buttercup yellow and hung with an antique chintz, which also drapes the armchair. The basin is set into an antique side table.

ABOVE RIGHT Irene's bedroom is at the opposite end of the house above the kitchen and is hung with black-and-white images by some of the photographers she commissioned when she was joint editor of French *Vogue*. White walls contrast with the rich colours and textures of curtains, upholstery, and the fabrics that drape the bed.

RIGHT The room is partitioned lengthways to make this small bathroom and shower room, and next to it, a walk-in wardrobe/closet where some of Irene's collection of ethnic and vintage clothing hangs on two tiers of rails. The bathroom contains some of her favourite shell-encrusted pieces, including mirrors, boxes, and even shelving.

ABOVE AND OPPOSITE All the bedrooms have high ceilings, and this one, which is across the landing from the blue bedroom, also has its original stone fireplace. Again, the painted decoration is by Giorgio, including the frieze of leafy garlands at cornice level. Furniture is a complete mix of periods and styles: an early-19th-century bookcase, which Giorgio painted white, an Empire bed, an Art Nouveau settee and two 20th-century chairs including an original Mies van der Rohe Barcelona chair upholstered in nut brown leather.

'I am Russian – in fact I am the great-niece of Trotsky – and Giorgio was Italian – so you have a bit of the gypsy, a bit of the baroque – and a lot of colour.' Irene's parents were Russian Jewish émigrés, who arrived in France before the war. Her father was a diamond dealer, and was sent to Auschwitz, where he died. Her mother evaded capture, and ran a shop selling lingerie after the war. Giorgio was born in Genoa, the son of an architect. 'My style is bohemian,' says Irene. 'Giorgio's classical.'

The effect of their decorative collaboration is rich and delectable, and seems to have matured over the decades such that all the different flavours have blended and harmonized. The Russian Constructivist chairs

lined up on a landing are as happy to sit next to an 18th-century painted commode as the Mies van der Rohe Barcelona chair is comfortable beside a mahogany Empire bed, and the slightly industrial pierced metal shades look entirely at home on the elaborately carved bases that predate them by at least two hundred years.

Irene still sometimes works with Yohji Yamamoto, still entertains friends from the world of fashion and glossy magazines, and still attends the catwalk shows in Paris. But this house is where her heart is – full of colour and collections, its mix of the antique and modern as casual and elegant as she, its walls saturated with memories.

DOUBLE VISION

If you believe in fate, you will be convinced that Nicole Albert and Michael Nunan were destined to live in Lagrasse. And not just in this particular French village in the Corbières hills near Carcassonne, but in this particular house. The story of how they came here has so many twists and turns that it does seem that circumstance was leading them here. Nicole says that coming to live in France was inevitable. Half-Belgian, half-English, she has been crossing the Channel since the age of three and is fluent enough to sound like a native. 'My parents had a house in the hills above Cannes,' she says. 'They were more chilled when we were in France, so it came to seem like a place where everything was more fun. As an adult, I dreamed of leaving London for the French countryside and setting up a retreat – yoga, Pilates, cookery, that kind of thing.'

ABOVE The terrace, with its view of the medieval bridge, is like a large extra living room in summer, and is furnished with a dining table, chairs, and sofas.

OPPOSITE ABOVE RIGHT AND BELOW LEFT The house is made up of two parts: a house on the street, and a house backing onto the river. Two covered wooden walkways, at first- and second-floor levels, link the houses across a small, cobbled courtyard.

OPPOSITE ABOVE LEFT Looking from the second floor of the river side, you can see the dining terrace of the first-floor river apartment.

OPPOSITE BELOW RIGHT From the street you would never guess that this house had so much internal space or views of the river.

PREVIOUS PAGES Nicole's house was built into the medieval defensive walls of Lagrasse, as can be seen in this view from the other side of the River Orbieu. Hers is the central building with white shutters. Her roof terrace, with its three stone pillars, once formed part of the walkway along the battlements. In summer the river retreats, but when it is in spate, her ground floor is liable to flood. The bridge is 12th century, and links the village with the monastery.

Instead, having studied history and history of art, Nicole apprenticed herself to a furniture restorer, then to an interior decorator, and finally found her métier working as a stylist, initially for Laura Ashley. 'Styling suited me better than interior decorating, where so much of the work is sitting at a desk. I prefer action.' But after 20 years of styling action, she had had enough. 'Michael and I were living in London, and I spent too much time in traffic jams. Michael had experience as a builder, and we thought "why not?" Let's go and make a new life for ourselves.'

Initially they looked near Cannes, in the part of France Nicole knew best, and where she still has many friends, but nothing they could afford suited them. So they began to look in less-expensive areas. 'We were booked to fly to Pau, but I read an article about it that put me off, saying that hunting was the most popular sport. I changed the flight to come to Carcassonne. A friend said we should visit Lagrasse and we immediately loved it. It ticked all the boxes – easily accessible, but also in the most stunning countryside, and on the banks of a beautiful river, the Orbieu.'

'We found a house in the village, and were a week away from the final, legal commitment to buy. Walking back from the *notaire*, I saw the boyfriend of a friend from England. It turned out the friend's sister had a house in the village and they asked us for dinner that night. Their house is diagonally opposite this one, which is how we saw the "For Sale" sign.' There follows a tale of French bureaucracy, a grumpy estate agent, last-minute flights, a single viewing and a rush decision. Suffice it to say that Nicole and Michael withdrew their offer on the first house, and instead became the owners of a house twice as big and half the price.

What they had not reckoned on was how much work it would take to bring out the potential they had seen in this ancient building. It had recently been a restaurant, and was

OPPOSITE A bedroom on the first floor overlooking the river has an internal balcony accessed up this miniature spiral staircase. Nicole inlaid the polished concrete floors with pebbles, and the painted table is from India.

RIGHT AND BELOW An alcove above a kitchen work surface displays a metal coffee set and a 19th-century watercolour. The French provincial dining table and chairs are set next to double doors that lead out onto an enclosed first-floor terrace in the space between the two houses. The window on the right looks over the cobbled courtyard below.

divided into small, dark rooms decorated in shades of brown, and had lost most of its original period features. 'Even some of the window glass was brown,' says Nicole. Two weeks before they moved in, the river flooded, leaving a deposit of damp and silt in the courtyard and ground-floor rooms. 'It wasn't attractive,' says Nicole.

Ten years on, Nicole has become reconciled to the occasional flood, and has organized the house to minimize its impact. And when you look through the windows at the back to see the wide, green water snaking past below, or step out onto the second-floor terrace to gaze at the view of the 12th-century hump-back bridge that links the village with the monastery rearing up from the rocks on the far side, or lie in bed with the window open listening to the creaking song of the marsh frogs, the inconvenience seems a small price to pay.

BELOW LEFT There are two spiral staircases in this house, three if you count the steps leading up to the bedroom gallery. The spiral staircase in the river-front house is original, probably medieval. This elegant sweep of stair was designed by Nicole and has hand-forged metal banisters and rail. It leads from the first-floor bedrooms of Nicole's part of the house to the living room.

BELOW Nicole's living room, dining room, kitchen, and study combined take up the whole of the second floor, underneath the huge, ancient beams of the house on the street. Furnishings are a confident mix of styles and periods. The space is flooded with daylight thanks to windows on three sides, overlooking the street and the inner courtyard, and looking up at the sky.

The house is terraced, but comes in two different helpings: the building at the front on the narrow, stone-paved street, and a larger building at the back that rises directly from the flat, wide shore of the river. Linking these front and back buildings, across a cobbled courtyard, are covered wooden walkways at first- and second-floor levels. The building on the street is where Nicole and Michael live, while the building at the back, which includes a spectacular roof terrace, has been converted into two holiday apartments.

This strange but appealing layout is a legacy of the fact that the riverside walls of the house are the old defensive walls of the medieval village and the roof terrace was once part of the

walkway along the top of the battlements. When building work began, Nicole and Michael tackled the back of the house first. Walls came down, floors were laid, and a second spiral staircase was constructed linking the two bedrooms in Nicole and Michael's part of the house with their open-plan living room and kitchen under the slope of the roof.

Michael took charge of the practicalities, Nicole of the aesthetics, finding old windows, reclaimed terracotta floor tiles, a stone basin, and antique metal grilles for windows and indoor railings. 'Sometimes I would come back with an old door and Michael would say "what am I meant to do with that?" But he would always find a way.' 'I would never again live in a house while doing so much building work,' she continues. 'We had endless dust, and some major disasters.' Now it is finished, and the rooms with their fresh, white paintwork are furnished with antique and vintage pieces. The visitors' books in the apartments are full of appreciative comments, and there is an air of peace and calm that makes it impossible to imagine the dirt and disruption it took to create this tranquil house.

ABOVE In a first-floor bedroom overlooking the river, Nicole has used an antique carved stone basin, probably from a church, and moulded a shaped splashback for it. The house had lost almost all of its original features when they bought it, but has regained a sense of history thanks to the use of reclaimed architectural fittings including doors, windows, fireplaces, hooks, and handles.

RIGHT Throughout the house Nicole's eye as a stylist is apparent in arrangements of disparate objects; here on a shelf behind her bed, a late-19th-century oil painting of a French town scene, and a metal sculpture of people she picked up for a few euros in a *vide grenier*.

OPPOSITE Nicole's bedroom is on the first floor, its window overlooking the village street. The door to the right of her bed leads out onto the walkway that links her part of the house with the first-floor holiday apartment. Another window to the right of her bed looks across the inner courtyard to the house on the river.

'I absolutely love this house,' says Nicole. 'I love the sounds of the river and the feeling of history, and I love the smell of thyme, pine, and rosemary when you walk in the hills.'

ALTERNATIVE LIVING

*F*or the past 25 years, Bert and Julia Huizenga have been living two quite different lives – a busy town life near Amsterdam, where both worked as teachers, he teaching geography, she teaching English language; and a quiet, country life on the very edge of a tiny village in rural France, complete with a garden, an orchard, outbuildings, a swimming pool, and a view of the distant Pyrenees. 'We eat different things, we see different friends, we even wear different clothes,' says Julia. 'It is wonderful to have the contrast, and a great privilege.'

PREVIOUS PAGES The Huizengas' farmhouse stands side-on to a lane. Facing the lane at the front and the distant Pyrenees at the back are these old farm buildings, with their unusual wooden verandah. Over the years, Bert and Julia have transformed this area in front of the house from barren, concrete farmyard to green lawn planted with olive, walnut, pine, and a palm tree.

ABOVE Wrought-iron entrance gates between elegant stone pillars once opened straight onto the farmyard. The sloping roof at the back of the house covers what was originally the granary, now converted to make a guest bedroom, bathroom, and study upstairs and a kitchen below.

OPPOSITE ABOVE LEFT TO RIGHT A bank of pink hydrangeas borders the house along the side of the lane. The farmhouse is double-fronted and dates from the early 18th century.

OPPOSITE BELOW LEFT TO RIGHT Doors, just seen on the right, open from the kitchen into an open barn, now used as a dining terrace, while a second door leads to the garden at the back of the house where Bert and Julia have planted an orchard of fruit trees (left). Looking from the same position in the other direction, there are steps at the side of the house that lead down from the French doors of the living room (right).

This is not privilege that has dropped into their laps; quite the contrary. The home the Huizengas have made for themselves in France is the result of hard work – years of hard work in fact. Nor is the journey between their two lives an easy one; 13 long hours of driving, fuelled by coffee and roadside picnics, and eased by music and the taking of turns at the wheel. The privilege of sitting back and enjoying the results of their labours is a relatively recent one. But now the house is finished, and Julia and Bert have both retired from full-time teaching, they can stay for as long as they like.

The property they bought all those years ago already had some fine features. A two-storey farmhouse, dating from the early 18th century,

RIGHT The kitchen, beneath the former granary, was once a wine cellar with an earth floor. Bert and Julia converted it, creating a big, open fireplace copied from one Julia saw in a magazine. The glazed wall cupboards with moustache hinges are made from old windows, and the kitchen cupboard doors are fashioned from old shutters.

BELOW Steps from the kitchen lead up into the living room through an ancient door, salvaged from the village church.

it retained its beautiful oak staircase, with two nicely proportioned rooms either side of it on both floors. At the back of the house, an extension with an earth floor housed a wine cellar and, above it, a granary. On the side of the house furthest from the lane there was an open barn, and this in turn was attached at right angles to a long, single-storey building, where the farmer kept his cows at one end, pigs at the other, and horses in between.

'It had always been a dream of ours to buy a house in France,' says Julia. 'We used to do a lot of mountain walking and camping, so it seemed obvious to look for a holiday home near mountains. As soon as we visited this area, we loved it. We signed up with a local estate agent and this was one of the first houses we viewed together. It was a mess – so much dirt and rubbish – and it didn't fit my criteria because I wanted somewhere surrounded by fields, with no cars and no neighbours, just the sound of birdsong.'

OPPOSITE AND BELOW Bert made this long table for the dining terrace that leads off the kitchen. The space is wired for electricity and is effectively an extension of the kitchen throughout the summer, and a favourite place for evening entertaining.

ABOVE AND LEFT At the far end of the dining terrace, two wicker loungers offer a shady place to relax with a view across the front garden. The old farm buildings on the right partially enclose the garden and, with their arched timbers and pantiled roof, are reminiscent of the design of a Roman country villa. A bench against the wall under the shade of the verandah holds a row of old earthenware pots (left).

While not completely isolated, the position of this property and its few hectares of land has other advantages. It is the first house you come to as you arrive from the nearest main road, in a hamlet with a handful of houses and a church, built on a ridge of land affording magnificent views across unspoilt countryside. While the farmhouse itself stands sideways onto the lane, the back of the long outbuilding, parallel to the lane, faces a line of snowy peaks that glitter in the strong, southern sunlight.

Like childbirth, or perhaps like having a tattoo (the second analogy is guesswork), it's easy to forget the pain of house renovation once you have achieved the desired result. Sitting on the vine-shaded terrace on a hot summer day, Bert explains that this was previously a steep slope, with nowhere to sit, let alone to put a table and chairs. 'I dug out the terraces myself,' he says, 'and I used the stone from where we lowered the walls of the outbuilding to make the retaining walls.' Julia remembers the physical effort, and the mud, dust, and chaos of living on a

ABOVE LEFT The farm building that adjoins the dining terrace was finished in time for Bert and Julia's eldest daughter's wedding. Bert removed part of the back wall of the building and replaced it with this row of reclaimed wooden windows that looks towards the Pyrenees.

LEFT The magnificent stone fireplace is 14th-century French, restored by Bert, and lends this space, once home to cows, a certain grandeur. The door leads out to a small terrace.

RIGHT Bert made the long table using floorboards from the old granary as its top. The double doors to the right of the fireplace open onto the dining terrace next to the kitchen.

'I used to find antique grates, fire dogs, fire irons and guards at *brocantes* and *vides greniers*, and this dealer would buy them from me to furnish his stock of old French fireplaces,' says Bert. 'He knew I was looking for a chimney piece and let me have this one for a very good price.'

building site. 'It was hard for the girls,' she says, 'because Bert and I were always busy. The first year we came they adopted a cat. The next year it was ducks. After that we allowed them to go camping with friends. Every year we would say that next summer we would take them to Portugal. But we always ended up coming here instead, and working on the house.'

Because it was built by hand, the terracing looks as though it has been there for generations. And this is true of all Bert and Julia's improvements. Bit by bit, they colonized the outbuildings. The wine cellar is now a generous, beamed kitchen with a big,

raised fireplace. Above, in the space that used to be the granary, there is a study, and a guest bedroom and bathroom. The kitchen leads into the open barn, which has become a dining terrace, its posts wrapped with sweet-scented jasmine. From here there is a door into the old cowshed, which has been transformed into a big, bright room with a peerless view, thanks to the partial removal of the back wall and the insertion of French doors and a row of casement windows. The pigsty, which they still call *la porcherie*, offers another sheltered table for dining and gazing into the distance. The farmyard, once

OPPOSITE The house is early 18th, possibly late 17th century, and one of its finest original features is the beautiful oak staircase that curves its way up to the first floor, and continues up to the attic. The bottom step is stone, dipped by generations of feet, and rises from a floor of old terracotta tiles. Bert and Julia have used paint to complement the interior architecture of the house, including a smoky blue for door surrounds, echoed here in a mid-20th-century painting.

RIGHT The library on the right-hand side of the staircase is lined with bookshelves on two walls, and also houses an upright piano. The fireplace is original and has a gracefully curved back. Bert's desk, piled with books, faces the fireplace.

barren concrete, is now an expanse of lawn, planted with olive, walnut, cypress, pine, and a palm tree, and edged by big terracotta pots of clipped box and tumbling geraniums.

Bert and Julia learned skills as they went, from plastering, to laying floors, to carpentry. Wherever possible they have used reclaimed building materials, such as the huge oak lintel for the kitchen fireplace that they found in one of their fields. 'All our friends in France know that we prefer old windows and doors, so when they are renovating, they offer to give us whatever they are replacing,' says Bert. The glazed kitchen cupboards, with their distinctive 'moustache' hinges, were once windows, and all the other kitchen cupboard doors are made from old shutters. They used floorboards from the hayloft for

the work surface, and to make the long table in the former cowshed. Wooden mangers became banisters for the landing of the back stairs. They even rescued two ancient doors from the village church, which they found propped outside, and that they were given official permission to re-use.

One of their most impressive additions is the handsome stone fireplace that dignifies the cowshed with its simple grandeur. It is 14th-century French, bought broken and painted bright blue from a dealer in Holland. 'I used to find antique grates, fire dogs, fire irons, and guards at *brocantes* and *vides greniers*, and this dealer would buy them from me to furnish his stock of old French fireplaces,' says Bert. 'He knew I was looking for a chimney piece and let me have this one for a very good price.'

OPPOSITE Bert and Julia's bedroom, above the living room, has two windows that overlook the garden at the front, and two windows at the side that look over the roof of the outbuildings and towards the mountains. Their bathroom opens directly off the bedroom, its Belfast sink backed by antique French tiles.

ABOVE In order to connect the main house with the extension at the back that was the old granary, a door through to it was made from this half landing. Facing the front of the house, Julia and Bert's bedroom and bathroom are on the right of the landing seen up the stairs.

ABOVE RIGHT AND BELOW RIGHT Across the landing from Bert and Julia's room is a second bedroom with a smaller back bedroom leading off it. These are the rooms used by their daughters as they were growing up, and which they still use now that they are both married. The floorboards are original, as is the fireplace.

LEFT To the right of Bert and Julia's bed is a glazed cupboard, its window lined with an old French lace curtain depicting swans. The mosquito net that shrouds the bed is hung from bamboo poles.

BELOW In this room there are two windows that overlook the distant mountains. Tendrils from the wisteria that clads the outside wall on this side of the house have a tendency to make their way inside.

OPPOSITE An extension with a sloping roof at the back of the house was originally a granary upstairs and a wine cellar below. Bert and Julia converted this extra space to make a kitchen, larder, and downstairs cloakroom, and on the first floor, this guest bedroom with adjoining bathroom. The walk-in shower is enclosed in a tiled pod, pierced with oblong windows, and the lavatory tucked away in the far corner is screened by thick canvas curtains.

Eight years ago, the eldest of their two daughters was married from here, and guests sat at long tables in front of this same fireplace. More recently, their second daughter chose the house as the venue for her wedding too.

They may not be 'in the middle of nowhere' as Julia had originally wanted, but the growl of a car is a rare event. Birdsong and the insistent trilling of cicadas are the only sounds. And when Julia sits at her grand piano, playing Brahms or Chopin, she says there are nightingales who join her with their own melodies. As for the neighbours, they have turned into very good friends.

BOXING CLEVER

Dutch artist Peter Gabrielse creates miniature three-dimensional spaces, framed rooms with tiny windows, and doors that often stand ajar. Furnishings are sparse – a chair or two, maybe a table, and perhaps some bundles of documents smaller than postage stamps, tied with thread. These shrunken worlds bear little relation to the cosy domesticity of a child's dolls' house, and even less to the ideal homes created by adult dolls' house enthusiasts. The microcosms created by Peter Gabrielse breathe a darker atmosphere, heavy with the promise of suspended belief and alternative reality – like stage sets waiting for slightly malevolent fairy actors.

PREVIOUS PAGES AND ABOVE
The roof and chimneys of the chateau can just be seen rising above trees as you approach along a country lane. Gateposts mark the entrance to the drive, which curves between an avenue of beech trees until it arrives at a second pair of gateposts that frame the symmetrical front facade. The grass in front of the house has just been mown, the cuttings swept into piles on the right-hand lawn, ready to be collected.

OPPOSITE ABOVE LEFT Carved into the stone lintel above the front door is the date 1727. The panelled double doors retain their original door furniture, including a metal cross-bar to secure them from the inside.

OPPOSITE ABOVE RIGHT
When Peter bought the house it was a farm, and had 11 *dépendances*, or outbuildings. Peter demolished the more modern of these, leaving only the ones with architectural merit, here an old greenhouse attached to the end of the remains of the earlier, 17th-century farmhouse.

OPPOSITE BELOW LEFT AND RIGHT A bench and a metal chair sit among Michaelmas daisies at the front of the house, placed to catch the morning sun. This half-timbered farm building in the grounds probably dates back to the 17th century, and houses the bed of an old cider press.

Much of the appeal of Peter Gabrielse's 'box sculptures' lies in the way they incorporate and recycle antique fragments, their frames made from the doors of 18th-century painted cupboards, pieces of panelling, or even carved and gilded tabernacles. Every component, from the full-scale curlicue on the wall to the mini console beneath it, has a patina of age, and no piece is complete without a softening of dust and a drape of cobweb. Peter is insistent about these last two elements, to the extent that his website advertises 'a strong dust and spider trend'. 'When I sell my boxes at art fairs,' he says 'people sometimes ask how I make the cobwebs! I find myself tempted to tell tales about journeys to remote monasteries in China where a rare and precious spider can be found and purchased at great expense.' The truth is more mundane – and simply a question of time.

The boxes developed as a creative sideline to Peter's job as a set designer for theatre and television. In the early 1990s, aged 55, he was made redundant and given what he describes as a 'generous pay-off'. Instead of splashing out on membership of a golf club, or tickets for a world cruise, he decided the time had come to buy instead of rent, and

OPPOSITE The kitchen is in one of the smaller rooms that run along the back of the house and which were once the domain of the servants. Its walls are hung with the 17th-century Delft tiles Peter collects, and Delft plates above. Through the door is the living room, where there is a sofa in front of a huge wood-burning stove. The floor in both these rooms is the original stone flags.

LEFT At the opposite end of the kitchen, an old glass-fronted cupboard holds saucepans and other kitchen paraphernalia, as well as some beautiful old creamware including tureens lined up along the top.

ABOVE The front door opens directly onto the broad, stone staircase where Peter stripped away layers of wallpaper to find the original paint scheme of arsenic green above a dado of ox-blood red. To the right is the showroom where he displays his boxes, and beyond that the workshop where he makes them. To the left is the living room, which leads into Peter's bedroom.

BELOW Looking across the end of the dining table, past the top of one of the 18th-century Dutch dining chairs, there is a view through the doorway into the kitchen. To the right of the doorway, a Norman grain chest supports sets of drawers, each containing some of the tiny elements Peter uses to create the miniature worlds of his box sculptures. Propped to the right are some fragments of gilded and embossed Spanish leather wall hangings, dating from the late 17th century, which Peter has restored and framed.

OPPOSITE The showroom, to the right of the front door, is where Peter displays his box sculptures, two of which can be seen mounted on the wall to the right of the door through to his workshop. The wires that dangle from their frames are for the integral lighting he designs to enhance their atmosphere. The coffee table is made from an engraved marble memorial stone mounted on a Perspex base.

chose an 18th-century village house on the border between Holland and Belgium, which he set about stripping of later decoration to create an interior rich with the texture of gentle decay. When not working on his house, he spent his time making boxes, and selling them to a growing clientele. Some years later Peter moved again, and a second 18th-century house was treated to the same process of anti-decorating. In 2000, he bought the house he has lived in ever since, an early-18th-century chateau at the western edge of Normandy.

It is the biggest of all the houses he has owned, and by far the most ambitious project. As you approach it, down a quiet country road that curves through undulating wheat fields, its chimneys and steeply pitched roof can just be seen rising among sheltering trees. An avenue of beech announces the entrance, and at its end the symmetrical facade is framed between two stone gateposts. Its exterior has all the restraint and elegance that Peter admires, and its interior all the patina and mystery of his boxes, plus a share of dust and spiders.

The front door opens onto a broad stone staircase. At the foot of the stairs, on either side, open doors reveal an *enfilade* of rooms. To the right is a showroom lined with Peter's boxes, and a view through to his studio workshop, originally a reception room, with next to it a smithy that was accessed from outside, both now knocked into one large space packed with tools and stacked with oddments of architectural salvage. The view from the staircase hall looking left is into the living room, through to Peter's bedroom, and beyond into a panelled room filled with bookshelves. 'The house is very cleverly designed,' Peter says. 'At the front are these large, formal rooms, but running behind them, along the back of the house, are the spaces that were used by servants.' Upstairs, the pattern is repeated, with four rooms along the front facade, and smaller rooms behind them.

It is a layout that works perfectly for modern living – the back rooms have been made into bathrooms and dressing rooms upstairs, and storage rooms, a utility room, a further bathroom, and a kitchen leading off the main living room downstairs. Peter lives on the ground floor. The first floor is reserved for guests, and above, accessed via a ravishing oval spiral of carved oak, are the attics. It's a big house for just one man and a cat, and visiting this top floor feels charged with the frisson of trespassing in rooms long undisturbed. It is exactly this sense of discovery, and of experiencing spaces redolent of the past, that Peter most enjoys and seeks to recreate in miniature.

He remembers these same feelings from childhood. 'We lived in an 18th-century townhouse in Zeeland, which had lots of little passages and cupboards to explore. I was the youngest of four and often left to my own devices.' His parents were antiques dealers, and his father restored furniture. Peter bought his first

OPPOSITE Peter has always used this ground-floor reception room as his bedroom, an arrangement that suits him all the better now he is in his eighties. His bed is to the right of the elegant, carved chimney piece, which holds a pair of carved wooden ecclesiastical urns. The panelled door to the left of the fireplace leads into two smaller rooms contained in one of the single-storey wings that flank the main body of the house.

ABOVE A detail of the granite fireplace in Peter's studio workshop, a large space he created by knocking through a reception room into the smithy that once occupied part of the single-storey wing on this side of the house. There is no central heating, only wood-burning stoves. Peter works on his boxes in the winter, as in the summer he is busy gardening.

RIGHT Suspended over the dining table is a Dutch brass chandelier. Dangling below it, a dolls' house version of it, of the sort Peter uses in his box sculptures, could easily be mistaken for a large spider.

antique with pocket money, aged 14. He still has it – a carved stone head, 16th-century, probably from a church. It sits among the groupings of objects he has accumulated over a lifetime of discerning acquisition, and that reveal certain aesthetic themes; among them a taste for the bold simplicity of Delftware, a delight in the humble elegance of country antiques, and a preference for design pre-1800.

The house itself looks as though it has been allowed to grow old graciously, without the indignity of later makeovers. Peter bought it from a family of farmers who, he says, 'did not appreciate its atmosphere'. They had boxed in all the panelling, blocked up the fireplaces, and lowered the ceilings in an attempt to make the rooms feel more modern and cosy. The process of removal was a thrilling one as old paint colours and wallpapers were disinterred, beams and mouldings released, and floors uncovered.

Tall and thin, with a beard that that would sit beautifully above an Elizabethan ruff, Peter still stands to work, whether he is restoring pieces of 17th-century Spanish leather wallcovering that he bought at an antiques fair and is framing

LEFT Peter's bed tucks neatly into an alcove created by two cupboards. The early-18th-century room layout, which placed large, elegant rooms along the front of the house, with smaller, interlinked rooms and a second staircase at the back for the discreet use of servants, suits modern requirements equally well. Peter's bathroom is in one of these service rooms, on the far side of a corridor behind his bedroom.

ABOVE At the top of the stairs, a mysterious trio of circles, engraved in the granite, could be a charm to ward off bad luck. The bench beneath the window on the half landing was made by Peter. A tapestry adds to the simple grandeur of the space.

OPPOSITE From the landing at the top of the stairs there is a view to either side through the four front bedrooms, now used as guest rooms. Downstairs the floors are stone; here they are parquet. The creamware plates hanging on the right of the door are antique, aside from the one at the bottom, which is a reproduction commissioned for Peter by a friend.

OVERLEAF This bedroom retains its original early-18th-century panelled cupboards and fireplace. Peter found the 19th-century wallpaper above the bed under later layers. The floor slopes such that two of the legs of the bed are propped on old books in order to save guests from rolling out.

for sale, or mitring the corners of a piece of 18th-century giltwood for another one of his boxes. 'The boxes keep me busy in winter,' he says. During the summer months Peter works in the garden and grounds, where wisteria cascades lavishly over outbuildings and the many trees he planted when he first came here are now well established, the foundations of the modern farm buildings he demolished gradually disguised by lawns and hedges. 'I have finished this house,' he says. 'I won't do another one.'

OPPOSITE The top floor has the feel of a lost domain, a series of rooms that have been left undisturbed, their plaster crumbling, their contents gathering dust and cobwebs. The landing is hung with old mercury glass mirrors in dark frames, and a table holds a collection of laboratory glass.

BELOW The stairs are an elegant, if dilapidated, oval spiral of oak, the linked arcading of their banisters a scaled-down version of the main staircase.

RIGHT Peter works at a bench in the window of his living room, restoring and framing pieces of antique gilded leather wall hanging he bought at auction. Some of the pieces he has finished are propped on the shelf of the cupboard, and on the floor to his left.

BELOW RIGHT In one of the attic bedrooms, a fragment of carved architectural woodwork has been placed above the mantelpiece. A rail attached to the ceiling beams supports a selection of rusted metal water bottles, the whole ensemble a picture of romantic decay.

'I have finished this house,' Peter says. 'I won't do another one.'

SOUTHERN LIGHT

*B*y the time a house is ready to be photographed, all the hard work has been done. All you see is the end result – flowers on the table, books on the bookshelves, cushions plumped, rugs straightened. The house of Sara Giunta and Jean-Luc Charrier, set on a quiet hillside in the Alpes-Maritimes, above the crowds, traffic, and all the hustle of Côte d'Azur glamour, seems so serene and mature that it is difficult to believe that 14 years ago, it was nothing more than an idea. 'It was a vineyard that had belonged to the same family since the 16th century,' says Sara. 'They still have a small house not far from here.'

PREVIOUS PAGES A broad, brick-paved terrace at the side of the house, shaded by a deep, metal pergola, is big enough for two tables that can be pushed together when family and friends gather. Above the terrace, behind the reclaimed railings, there is a swimming pool.

OPPOSITE ABOVE LEFT AND RIGHT The view looking down on the dining terrace from the lawn that surrounds the pool. Most of the architectural elements, outside as well as in, are reclaimed, including the large herringbone bricks that pave the terrace outside the kitchen, and the hexagonal clay tiles that pave a second terrace to the side of the garden at the front of the house.

OPPOSITE BELOW LEFT AND RIGHT Even the swimming pool looks like a feature in the garden of a Roman villa thanks to its construction using reclaimed stone. The aged herringbone brick paving continues around the house to the front facade, where tall metal windows and French doors open onto lawn and trees. The pots are antique, as are the chairs.

ABOVE LEFT AND RIGHT Double doors, protected by exterior shutters, open onto the garden from Sara's bedroom. The main entrance of the house is through the plain, rear facade where a pair of 18th-century double doors open into a small staircase hall. The glazed double doors opposite lead down into the living room.

When they bought the land as a building plot, Sara and Jean-Luc were living over their shop in nearby Valbonne, in an 18th-century townhouse with a courtyard garden. It is still their shop, but has an extra floor of showroom since they moved out, giving them more space to display the sophisticated mix of furnishings that characterize *La Maison de Charrier*: 18th-century panelling and cupboards with original paint, dark oil portraits, glass and mottled mirrors, antique chairs and sofas upholstered in undyed linens, and a small selection of elegant contemporary pieces including the fine, pale, feather-light pottery of Astier de Villatte, which is made in this area.

Their home is a refined and beautifully edited version of the shop. At the top of a drive lined with cypress trees, you arrive at a plain facade where a pair of double doors open into a simple hall. Facing you are glazed doors and steps leading down into a big, white room lit by French doors onto a garden, and a row of windows with fine glazing bars, the size and style of which give the space the feel of an 18th-century orangery.

PREVIOUS PAGES AND OPPOSITE The living and dining room is L-shaped, and wraps around the kitchen. Furnishings are a mix of antique pieces, including the chandeliers, contemporary pieces, like the floor lamp, and contemporary pieces with a period feel, such as the sofa, upholstered in natural linen from their shop, *La Maison de Charrier*. The internal features – the floor tiles, the ceiling beams and planking, the glazed doors, and the 17th-century chimney piece – are all reclaimed.

RIGHT Glazed double doors link the dining area with the kitchen next door. A mix of similar, but not exactly matching, 19th-century French chairs is ranged around the table ready for guests, including five of Jean-Luc and Sara's seven children.

'Proportions are so important,' says Sara. 'A building must look beautiful when empty.'

LEFT The tall, metal-framed windows, which give this room the bright, airy elegance of an 18th-century orangery, have internal shutters that help to retain warmth in winter and to keep the room cool and shaded in summer. The door to the right of the chimney piece leads to Sara's bedroom, bathroom, and dressing room. Above it is an oval aperture cut to fit an 18th-century window.

And here is that same mix of antiques and newer pieces, linen upholstery in shades of pearl and silvery grey, and Astier de Villatte candlesticks lined up on the mantelpiece.

The contents reflect the style of the shop, but the architecture is grander. 'As well as being antiques dealers and interior decorators, we specialize in the restoration of old houses,' says Sara. 'When it came to building something completely new, we used the same skills and expertise.' Limited by planning restrictions, which stipulated a maximum footprint and height for the building, they decided to give the five first-floor bedrooms and two bathrooms more modest proportions in favour of high ceilings throughout the ground floor. This floor comprises the large L-shaped living and dining room that wraps around the kitchen, and also Sara's bedroom and bathroom, and their seven-year-old son Lupo's bedroom, all of which lead off the main room. 'Proportions are so important,' says Sara. 'A building must look beautiful when empty.'

Certainly they have created a series of beautiful spaces in these light-filled downstairs rooms, but they have also built a house that, like its furnishings, combines the old with the new.

THIS PAGE AND OPPOSITE ABOVE RIGHT
The back wall of the kitchen is decorated with
18th-century geometric wall tiles and the room is
furnished with a 17th-century oak table. The stone
sink beneath the window is antique and the waist-
height stone mortar to its left came from a convent.
To the right of the table a section of timber flooring
lifts up to reveal stairs down to the wine cellar.

OPPOSITE Sara's ground-floor bedroom is housed in its own wing, which projects into the garden and has windows on three sides. Her four-poster bed is constructed around four 18th-century wooden architectural columns, probably from the interior of a church, and that retain the rubbed remains of their original paint. Framed in a clear box on the desk at the end of her bed is a letter from Pope Pius V to a member of her family.

RIGHT This large, ground-floor room, with its wall of painted 18th-century panelling, was originally designed to be an office, but has instead become seven-year-old Lupo's bedroom, where tables are spread with a miniature world of the Lego models he has made, most recently a spaceship. Vintage model aeroplanes are suspended from the ceiling.

'As well as being antiques dealers and interior decorators, we specialize in the restoration of old houses,' says Sara. 'When it came to building something completely new, we used the same skills and expertise.'

OPPOSITE Next to Sara's bedroom is her bathroom, where the end wall is clad in antique panelling, into which has been fitted the tap/faucet, and behind which the plumbing pipes are hidden. The roll-top bathtub and the marble washbasin are both antique.

ABOVE Planning restrictions dictated the height of the house, and Jean-Luc and Sara decided to sacrifice ceiling height upstairs in favour of grand proportions for the downstairs rooms. As a result, the upstairs has a more rustic feel and furnishings to match, including a Moroccan tufted rug on the landing. Windows are also smaller, such as this round window set high in the wall of one of the shower rooms.

Starting from scratch has enabled them to work around architectural antiques, creating openings to fit an 18th-century front door and reclaimed windows, cladding walls with panelling, and constructing a chimney breast around a superb stone chimney piece that dates from the 17th century. Also reclaimed are the clay tiles in shades of soft gold and apricot, which spread their variegated blush across every floor upstairs and down. Handles, window fastenings, shutters, wall tiles, ceiling beams, wardrobe doors, outdoor paving, and even the kitchen sink, all are antique.

The floor may be antique, but it is also heated. History and comfort, patina and state-of-the-art plumbing, this house seems to have it all. As Sara sweeps from room to room, organizing lunch and arranging flowers, while Jean-Luc scans his laptop at the table on the shady terrace outside the kitchen, and Lupo builds a Lego spaceship in his panelled bedroom, their life looks like one of picture-perfect privilege. Which it is. But it is also the result of passion and talent, of years of experience, and sheer, determined, doggedly enthusiastic effort.

Joining Jean-Luc at the table outside, Sara reminisces. They met in the late 1990s when she was furnishing and restoring a house, and started visiting his antiques shop. 'Jean-Luc and I had very different journeys. I was born in Sicily into a family of doctors, and lived in

Rome, then Tangiers. Jean-Luc's mother was Italian, but his father was French and he was brought up here and studied history of art. We made a strong connection, and discovered we shared similar and complementary tastes, and a passion for antiques and design,' says Sara. Both had young children from previous marriages – she four boys, he a boy and a girl – but they decided to open a shop together. 'We left our marriages with nothing, and started from scratch. We found the house where our shop is and worked on it every day until eight or nine at night. When we opened, we had a small stock, but our first customer was an American – she bought lots of things and came back the next day with a big bouquet of flowers to wish us luck. Not long after that I found my first client, who came in saying he needed a new carpet, and ended up employing me to redesign and decorate his whole house. He was my angel.'

Over the years since, they have gathered a loyal following, including the rich and famous about whom they are admirably discreet. And at the same time, they have been working on their own project, this house, sticking to a strict budget, and progressing as funds allowed. When Lupo was born, they adjusted their plans to make the room that was going to be their office into a bedroom for him. Having bought the plot in 2002, it took another four years of planning and ten years of construction before it was finished. Even now there is the odd wire protruding from a wall, waiting for the right light fitting.

Today is a family lunch, a gathering of five of their seven children including Lupo – one who works in finance, one an actor and comedian, one an animator, one a professor of philosophy. After lunch, they all jump in the pool. A privilege they probably appreciate all the more for having had to wait.

ABOVE AND BELOW LEFT
Jean-Luc has his own bedroom upstairs, under the slope of the roof, where he keeps his beloved bicycle, plus stacks of bike magazines piled up on both sides of the bed. His love of antiques is equally apparent in a room that represents his personal passions. The bench at the foot of the bed is 17th century, and there is an 18th-century, articulated wooden figure of a saint sitting at the top of an antique stepladder overlooking it.

In stark contrast, a rubber Mickey Mouse is caught mid-stride in a glass dome on the painted sideboard opposite the bed.

OPPOSITE An antique painted canvas screen forms a gorgeously decorative bedhead, and on it is suspended an exquisitely carved wooden figure of the crucified Christ, intensifying the mix of the sacred and the profane in this highly individual room.

Thekla and Luc Benevello knew what they were letting themselves in for when they decided to buy La Queurie, partly because they had restored old houses before. But this was the biggest and bravest acquisition to date – a 15th-century manoir, with an accumulation of farm buildings, surrounded by farmland, and edged by a river. They also knew they could not afford to restore it fully. The plan was to consolidate the medieval house and save it from further deterioration, and also to restore the older outbuildings, and to convert the largest of the barns into a home. 'I agreed to go through it all again because it was going to be the last house we rescued,' says Thekla. 'It was the place we planned to settle for the rest of our lives.'

PREVIOUS PAGES Approaching the farm buildings down a track off a country road, the pointed turret and steep roofs of the *manoir* rise up on the right, while the converted 18th-century barn where Thekla lives is straight ahead. Behind the hedge on the right is a flower and vegetable garden planted and tended by Thekla, who studied horticulture as a mature student.

ABOVE From the outside, the barn that is now Thekla's home looks much the same as it did when it housed animals.

OPPOSITE ABOVE LEFT TO RIGHT An ancient stone basin in a wall of one of the barns. The roofs of the outbuildings have all been repaired and restored using old pantiles. The door to the wing of the 15th-century *manoir* where the farmer's family lived.

OPPOSITE BELOW LEFT TO RIGHT There is a carved ogee above the main entrance to the *manoir* that opens directly onto a stone spiral staircase enclosed in the turret. The buildings have all been made safe and weatherproof, and are supported by wooden buttressing where necessary.

RIGHT At the far end of the barn from the kitchen is a self-contained suite of rooms that Thekla makes available for guests. In the living room, an extra divan/box spring bed that doubles as a sofa when not in use is draped with an antique hemp sheet, and made comfortable with cushions. The wall behind the bed is panelled with the same Normandy oak used for the floors.

BELOW In front of the wall that hides the stairs to the mezzanine is an antique sleigh bed that Thekla inherited from her grandfather. Flowers are from the garden and surrounding meadows. Most of the walls are limewashed in a pale stone, but this section of wall has been painted charcoal grey.

OPPOSITE All the antiques here are inherited pieces, including the armoire against the back wall that Thekla uses to store bedlinen, just as it has always been used. Doors and windows respect the placing of the original openings, and along the back wall of the barn form tall slots that extend almost to the ceiling. The bedroom is above this near end of the room.

For the first two years, the farm remained tenanted and was home to a dairy herd of 200 cows. In 2007 the farmer moved out and work began. Five years on, Luc Benevello, a photographer specializing in portraits, compiled a book entitled *La Queurie 2005–2010, Le Début de l'Aventure* documenting their progress in words and photographs. He writes beautifully and poetically about the responsibility of becoming the caretakers of a place with 600 years of history behind it, about the need for 'modesty' in the face of such a task, and about the insignificance of their own contribution in the context of the long life, past and future, of such venerable buildings. He also tells how the roof of the largest barn collapsed just 15 days after they signed the purchase contract, and talks of how they often felt like 'throwing in the sponge' and giving up.

OPPOSITE Set in the middle of the barn, beneath the first-floor pod that encloses Thekla's bedroom and bathroom, is the living area. The buttoned, modular sofas, upholstered in grey chenille, belonged to Thekla's parents and date from the 1970s. Facing them is an Eames-style leather armchair. On the left, a doorway opens into another guest bedroom and adjoining bathroom.

LEFT The tall windows and French doors of the living area frame a charred oak sculpture by the French artist Christian Lapie, who is a friend. On the other side of their dark silhouettes, the land slopes down to the banks of the River Orne, which in parts is wide and deep enough for summer swimming.

BELOW Thanks to the careful positioning of openings between rooms along the front of the barn, when the sliding doors are not shut there is a view from one end to the other, here looking past the kitchen on the left, past the door to the internal utility room, through the central living area, and into the suite of rooms at the far end. On the right are oak cupboards, built into the thickness of the wall, but also projecting slightly for a sculptural effect.

Before, during, and after photographs depict the transformation of the concrete farmyard into flower beds, grass, and gravel, and the demolition of the modern farm buildings; the new roofs using old tiles; the clearing and mending, the propping and reinforcing, and the putting right after years of neglect. In 2011, Luc and Thekla were finally ready to begin making a new home for themselves and their two children inside the soaring spaces of the barn, one end of which had been stables, while the other end originally housed a massive granite cider press.

Their principle was one of respect for the past, but also of care for their impact on the present. 'We tried to waste as little as possible,' Thekla says. 'We re-used everything, and we used local Normandy oak for the floors and cut the planks to follow the line of the tree trunks. It makes laying the floors much more difficult and time-consuming, but Luc did it all himself.' The double-height ceiling is planked and insulated with hay bales, and the thick stone walls have an extra layer thanks to an intra-wall heating system from Germany.

ABOVE AND RIGHT Looking across the kitchen table to French doors through which there is a view of the bend of the river, at a place where it broadens and the bank flattens, making it ideal for swimming. Part of the working area of the kitchen slots underneath a central pod that encloses a utility room below and an office above. The oak stairs lead up to the office and to Thekla's bedroom and bathroom above the living room.

Hot water and heating are fuelled by a biomass boiler that uses off-cuts from the local sawmill. 'I buy the chippings "wet", which is even cheaper, and dry them in one of the barns,' says Thekla. 'But the house is so well insulated, it costs very little to keep it warm.'

The interior of the barn is strikingly plain, the stark modernity given character and warmth by the textures of lime plaster, and oak. Windows reflect the original openings, reaching from floor to ceiling in four columns of glass along the back of the building, giving

ABOVE The central pod that forms the back wall of the working area of the kitchen is entirely clad in old roof slates reclaimed from some of the newer farm buildings that were demolished. Breakfast for guests includes a glossy brioche loaf, fetched fresh every morning from the local bakery, and eggs from Thekla's hens.

ABOVE RIGHT Thekla's collection of turquoise pottery, stored in the cupboards built into the wall, is set against a background of grey paint such that the cupboards look just as handsome open as they do closed.

OPPOSITE Beneath the oak treads of the stairs to Thekla's office and bedroom, an inherited 17th-century still-life painting is propped next to a collection of old green glass bottles that were once used for wine.

views across the sunken path of the River Orne to the fields and hills beyond. If you enter through the middle door from the old farmyard on the other side, you find yourself in the central living room, its ceiling formed by the white box that encloses Thekla's bedroom and bathroom. To the right, a corridor leads to a bedroom on a platform above its own living room and bathroom. To the left, past a central utility room, is the double-height kitchen, its working core tucked underneath a study suspended above it like the bridge of a ship. There is another downstairs bedroom with its own bathroom leading off the living room on the river side of the barn.

Lines are straight, vistas from one end of the building to the other are long, and the verticality of the proportions is preserved throughout by a first floor that is partial and fragmented.

Thekla and Luc worked on the design together, and their care for every detail shows, whether in the way the oak kitchen cupboards stand just proud of the wall into which they are fitted, or the choice and placing of hooks in the bathrooms. Some of the furniture is modern, some vintage, like the 1970s sofas that belonged to Thekla's parents. But there are also inherited antiques, which look particularly striking in this contemporary setting.

It is an impressive creation for two people with no training in architecture or interior design, though Thekla admits these are subjects she would love to have studied had not the education system in her native Germany insisted on high-level maths in order to pursue them. Instead, she came to Paris where she found work designing on magazines. After meeting Luc, having their two children, and moving out

of the city, she studied horticulture and garden design, and these remain a passion. La Queurie has benefitted from her knowledge, its buildings now edged by lush planting, its land enhanced by more than a hundred new trees, and 2km/1¼ miles of new hedging.

Before the barn was completely finished, Luc became ill. He died in 2015. Even though both the children have since left home to study, Thekla decided to stay on, finish the project, and live the life she and Luc thought they would share in this idyllic place. 'All the land is farmed organically,' she says. 'I only eat meat from my own chickens, who also give me eggs every day.' She spends as much time as she can in the garden: 'There is nothing I love more than working outside,' she says. She also offers bed and breakfast in her two spare bedrooms, and often has guests who are friends, as well as guests who pay. 'It is the most wonderful place to live. The light is beautiful, the air is so fresh. You can swim in the river,' she says. 'I am very, very lucky to be here. This is my paradise on earth. Luc felt the same about it.'

OPPOSITE At the kitchen end of the barn, the ceiling is at its full height, which, combined with the tall French windows with their gently arched tops, gives the space an uplifting verticality. The thickness of the walls, sturdy already but increased by the inclusion of intra-wall heating embedded in the lime plaster, can be seen from the depth of the window rebates.

LEFT The advantage of the heating system, which is powered by a biomass boiler, is its efficiency and the even distribution of heat. The disadvantage is that pictures are better propped than hung – here a study for a sculpture by Christian Lapie.

ABOVE There is a monastic simplicity to the design of the interior, which can also accommodate the slight messiness of life, such as this wall of books in the central living area. The view past it is towards the kitchen.

LEFT Thekla uses the two bedrooms at the far end of the barn from the kitchen to house guests. This bedroom adjoins the living area, and the view from its open door is towards the kitchen table. Antique pieces are shown to good advantage in the chaste, architectural setting, here an 18th-century painted commode and a mirror from the same century, both inherited.

BELOW LEFT AND RIGHT In the same bedroom, lime green linen covers the duvet, and matches the upholstery of the bed itself. The ceiling is full height, but bookshelves sit above the bathroom behind the dark grey wall on the right, a colour that is echoed by the slate tiling that lines the wet-room shower. In the wet room, an internal window of frosted glass looks onto the corridor that leads to the second downstairs bedroom.

OPPOSITE Set on a mezzanine floor, accessed by a narrow, slot staircase, this is the bedroom that sits above the living room with the sleigh bed and armoire. The floor is oak from local forests, and has been cut to follow the line of the tree trunks in order to minimize wastage. As well as being environmentally friendly, it gives the floors a pleasing irregularity, while being more difficult and time-consuming to install than standard planks. Luc laid floors in this way throughout the barn, a true labour of love.

'It is the most wonderful
place to live. The light is
beautiful, the air is so fresh.
You can swim in the river.'

CREATIVE
COLLABORATION

*A*rriving at D'Une Ile is like wandering onto a stage
set for a period drama, a pastoral love story
starring a rosy-cheeked milkmaid and a poetic shepherd.
The mise-en-scène is a gathering of crooked stone
cottages huddled around a sloping village green, their
walls the colour of apricots, their clay-tiled roofs padded
with moss, their doors wreathed with old-fashioned roses,
and their small casement windows shadowed by shutters
and hung with curtains of gathered white muslin. Behind
the cottages, the tall trees of an ancient woodland loom
up to create a dark, theatrical backdrop.

PREVIOUS PAGES Built on the
edge of an ancient forest as housing
for the woodsmen of a large estate,
this rustic hamlet could not look less
like a hotel. The oldest of the buildings
is the one on the near left, which is
probably 16th century, and is now
home to Sofie and Michel, who own
and run the hotel. The rest of the
buildings are 17th century, and the
barn on the right, used as a summer
bar, is 19th century.

OPPOSITE PAGE This is the front of
the building in which Sofie and Michel
live (above left). Its interior design is
their next project. At its far end, a
covered verandah currently shelters

two antique tubs (below left).
Michel is considering placing them in
an adjacent meadow, so that guests
can bathe alfresco. At the other end
of this verandah, a vintage table holds
flower pots and flowers in a glass jar
(below right). The picture hung on
the wall above turns the space into
an impromptu outdoor room. An old
wooden cartwheel is propped against
one of the end walls.

ABOVE The row of cottages at right
angles to Sofie and Michel's house
originally incorporated a communal
kitchen with a lean-to bread oven that
can just be seen to the right of the
chairs and tables.

However, unlike a movie set, or a model village, or Marie-Antoinette's *hameau*, this is somewhere you can immerse yourself, because more than just a bucolic fantasy, D'Une Ile is also a hotel and a home. After you have found it, buried deep in the gentle hills of Normandy's Le Perche, down a lane, past a pond, then through an orchard, and have parked in the grassy car park, you realize there are no signs pointing to 'Reception', no desk with telephones, and no forms to be filled in. Your passport won't be taken nor will you be given a room key. Instead you will be warmly greeted by either Michel or Sofie, the young Dutch couple who own and run it. They will usher you into the big, beamed dining room, and offer you something to drink, and then they will show you to the door of the cottage where you will be staying, a door with no lock.

At this point, there will be another surprise. Because inside these old cottages is a series of interiors as unexpectedly contemporary as they are creative. Three of the five buildings are divided into nine guest rooms, some with more than one bedroom, which when fully occupied can accommodate 28 guests. And although their exteriors are homogeneous, each is very different once you step behind its front door. One has a sunken bathtub in the corner, a separate shower room concealed behind a wired-glass partition, and a suitcase gramophone with a supply of vinyl LPs, while another boasts a chaise longue in pink plastic, the frame of an old hospital screen as a clothes rail, and a bed set into a wooden platform painted mint green. One has a manger along the wall above the bed, and a claw-foot tub set in front of a huge fireplace and bread oven.

LEFT When they bought the property, all character had been stripped away from these old cottages, leaving a blank canvas on which Sofie and Michel could impose their own ideas. Thanks to their creativity, they have come up with a series of interiors that are all quite different. The rooms on these pages are adjacent, and have a simple, rustic, vintage style, while being comfortable and well equipped. Although there is no wardrobe, there are plenty of wooden clothes hangers.

OPPOSITE An old kitchen cupboard at the foot of the bed contains a kettle and everything needed to make tea. The wastepaper basket is a large vintage tin with a fitted lid. The chair is one of many mid-century modern pieces, some of which are available to buy. None of the doors have keys.

'I phoned Sofie and told her I had found paradise,' says Michel.

TOP Next to the barn, this building was once a cowshed, with a hayloft above, but is now the dining room, with tables outdoors and inside, to be used according to the weather.

ABOVE AND RIGHT The stone feeding trough along the back wall serves as temporary storage for the local fruits and vegetables Michel uses to prepare meals in the adjacent kitchen. Guests dine by fire and candlelight, and on dark mornings the candles are also lit for breakfast. Michel is a talented chef, and dining is one of the great pleasures of a visit here.

One has a dining area on a mezzanine floor up in the rafters. And one – the most recently completed – has bedrooms in pods made from plywood and inserted into its shell at disconcerting angles.

All offer comfort as well as visual impact, and are furnished with vintage pieces from Fabriek NL, mixed in with things found at *brocantes* and *vide greniers*, and works by Dutch artists such as the sculptor and furniture maker Just van der Loos. But what is most unexpected about these fresh, modern spaces is that almost all the hard graft, the stripping out, the tiling, the sanding, even the plastering, was done by

Sofie and Michel themselves. Which just shows how deceptive appearances can be; both tall, slender, and good-looking, you can more easily imagine them on a catwalk than wielding drills and hammers.

The hotel opened in 2012, but the story of its creation began a couple of years before when Michel and Sofie were based in Amsterdam. Still only in their mid-twenties, Michel was making a living as a singer and composer, and Sofie, who had graduated from the prestigious Amsterdam Fashion Institute, was working as a freelance graphic designer, as well as teaching, and trying her hand at interior decoration. 'But we were restless,'

ABOVE There is a playful, youthful feel to these interiors that is given full rein in the 19th-century barn next to the dining room. This big, open-sided space is used as a summer bar, and comes into its own for weddings and parties. Beer stands lined up behind the wooden counter, beneath a reproduction of a Dutch old master portrait, ready for guests to arrive.

RIGHT AND OPPOSITE The barn is also the wood store, as well as the repository for furnishings that are waiting to be mended, or adapted, and for things such as this reproduction chandelier that have no other place. A section of old staircase appears to wind up to a platform, but the notice behind the stuffed stoat warns 'No entry'.

146

says Michel. 'We wanted to live a different life. And we came up with the idea of moving, ideally to somewhere sunny, and starting a business of our own, perhaps a restaurant. We both have a great interest in good food and wine – I come from a family of wine merchants – and I am passionate about cooking. I came across this place by chance, driving through France on my way to see Sofie who was staying with her parents in the south. There were two other people interested in buying it, so I had to make an instant decision. I phoned Sofie and told her I had found paradise. She agreed that we should try to buy it before she had even seen it.'

Over the next few days Michel taught himself Excel, and with the help of friends who ran hotels in Amsterdam, they wrote a business plan in double-quick time, and persuaded a small group of investors to back them. The purchase went ahead, and they moved to France during a long, hot summer. The buildings date from the 17th century, and originally housed the estate woodsmen and their

'For a year and a half, we had no heating or hot water,' says Sofie. 'We bought a brazier that we used to huddle around, and as soon as we had put showers and hot water into the guest rooms, we would rush in and use them the minute guests had left.'

ABOVE The most recently converted of the cottages has been completely transformed by the insertion of a series of plywood pods. Entering through its front door there is a separate bathroom to the left and this bedroom pod to the right, which incorporates a galley kitchen along the outside of its far wall.

OPPOSITE The biggest window of this ground-floor bedroom pod faces the fireplace. Inside, there is just space for a large double bed and a bedside table. Internal curtains can be pulled across the window for privacy.

RIGHT From inside the bedroom pod looking out, there is a view of the sitting-room area and the large open fireplace. The staircase next to it leads up to a further three bedrooms, two of them also inside plywood pods.

ABOVE Upstairs, the bedroom pods are linked by walkways with metal railings that look down over the room below. The smallest of these is the pod seen on the right, which has a sloping roof. The pod on the left has walls partially made of frosted glass and contains another double bed.

OPPOSITE The bathroom for these pod bedrooms is also characterized by the used of plywood, with its warm, honey colour, and the strong, organic patterns of its wavering grain. The sunken tub is reached by climbing a plywood staircase, and there is also a walk-in shower. All in all, these are rooms probably best suited to guests who are reasonably agile.

families, plus a few cows, pigs, and sheep. In the 1970s, another Dutch man had attempted, and failed, to turn the place into a golf resort. It had subsequently been used as a holiday home and had not been well maintained. Sofie says the interiors were 'super-ugly with horrible staircases, and vinyl wallpaper'. Undeterred by the lack of running water, and with the energy and enthusiasm of youth, they set to work.

Sunshine and help from visiting friends kept them going, but then came winter. 'For a year and a half, we had no heating or hot water,' says Sofie. 'We bought a brazier that we used to huddle around, and as soon as we had put showers and hot water into the guest rooms, we would rush in and use them the minute guests had left.' Ever since they opened, the rooms have never been empty for long, as word spread of the dinners prepared by Michel using locally

sourced meat, fish, and vegetables, the excellent *vins natures*, the unusual beauty of the place, and its relaxed, friendly feel.

The only remaining corner that has not been transformed is the biggest of all the buildings. This is Michel and Sofie's home. It is lovely as it is, with its spacious, high-ceilinged main room and broad stone fireplace, but it is not ready to be photographed. They have all kinds of plans for it – they haven't decided which they like best – but the design might include a section of glass flooring, and possibly more plywood. Whatever they decide, you can be certain it will be imaginative and handsome. Nor would you be surprised, once it is all done, to hear that they are moving on to their next project somewhere else in France, or even further afield. You can be equally certain you will want to visit if you can.

OPPOSITE This suite of rooms, which comprises two bedrooms and a bathroom in between, is accessed up a stone staircase at the side of the row of cottages, and is entered at ground level from the back. This, the bigger of the two bedrooms, has a mint green platform bed, a chaise longue, and the metal frame of a vintage hospital screen (not shown) hung with coat hangers as a clothes rail.

ABOVE LEFT AND RIGHT The bathroom adjacent to the bedroom with the green platform bed has a light suspended from an antler, while in another bathroom, an antler is suspended from the ceiling to be used as a clothes rail. The forest adjacent to the cottages is full of deer, and also wild boar.

RIGHT In this bedroom, which is above the bathroom in the suite of plywood pods, the door is wired glass, allowing light onto the walkways that link these first-floor rooms. The mid-century modern and vintage furnishings of the rooms, here an elegant Danish chair, and a small vintage desk from a primary school, change regularly as they are sold and moved around.

SIMPLE
PLEASURES

*T*he restoration of an old building is often a process of subtraction – removing later accretions to reveal original features, stripping back to find the character and history that have been masked. But sometimes it is the reverse. When Claude and Bénédicte Petit (not their real names) decided to buy a house in Provence, the buildings they bought were architecturally undistinguished and uninhabitable. The metamorphosis has been so complete that you need to pore over before and after pictures in order to believe that this expansive, apparently 18th-century house was once a collection of barns, stables, and a simple mas, or farmhouse, with no bathroom.

PREVIOUS PAGES At the back of the house, which faces south, three plane trees create pools of shade in the raked gravel. The largest of these, the one in the foreground, was already here, but the other two were craned in and planted as mature trees. At the near end of the house, a long, covered balcony shelters the dining terrace outside the kitchen.

OPPOSITE From the upper terrace, there is a glorious view across the pool, past olive and fig trees, towards the craggy outline of the Alpilles, a range of mountains where the family often go walking. The terrace is overlooked from inside by the main bedroom and bathroom, and a door at the far end opens into the office,

a private sanctuary on the other side of the main bedroom. When they bought the buildings, this view was obscured by a barn. Fortunately, they were given planning permission to demolish it.

ABOVE LEFT The architect Alexandre Lafourcade has transformed a series of undistinguished farm buildings in a magnificent location, and created an elegant house that looks as though it has been here for two centuries. The illusion is enhanced by his inclusion of architectural antiques, such as the front door.

ABOVE RIGHT On the far side of the terrace on the south side of the house, four old mulberry trees form an umbrella of shade over a metal table and chairs – a favourite place to eat lunch.

As buyers relatively unconstrained by timing or budget – he has a high-profile role in the French press, she is younger, his second wife, and they have six grown-up children between them – you might wonder why the Petits chose to take on such a full-scale renovation when there must have been plenty of other lovely Provençal houses to tempt them. Bénédicte says that they were initially looking for 'a small property that did not require too much work', but that when they came to see this semi-derelict farm, they were so 'dazzled' by its setting that they changed their minds.

Of course they were right, as is obvious now the transformation is complete. After all, you can work magic on a building, as long as you have building permits and funding, but you cannot move mountains, and gone are the days when a disfiguring village or an awkwardly

placed hill could be swept away to improve the prospect. This site already had its mountains, Les Alpilles, and they were in just the right place, their craggy, serrated outline silhouetted against the seamless blue of the Provençal sky on the south side of the house. The house is surrounded by 100 hectares of its own unspoilt farmland, green with trees, bright with wildflowers, and busy with wildlife; there is an electric fence to keep out the foraging *sangliers*.

Now it was just a question of creating a house worthy of the location. The agent recommended the architectural firm of Bruno and Alexandre Lafourcade, based nearby in St-Rémy-de-Provence, and renowned for their pristine and historically sensitive work on grand 18th-century houses. The collaboration was an immediate success. 'We wanted a house that would be relaxing, serene, and a haven for

ABOVE AND OPPOSITE The owners' brief was for an interior of simple luxury – comfortable, free from clutter, and capacious enough to accommodate their extended family, and the finished design was achieved in collaboration with decorator Karine Stoufs. The living room fills one end of the house and has its own covered terrace accessed through three sets of French doors. Its colour scheme was inspired by the black circle painting by Fabienne Verdier, which hangs on the wall between the two front windows. The other two abstract paintings are by Jean-Pierre Pincemin. The straight-sided armchairs and occasional tables are from Poliform. The owner found the flooring, which is *pierre de carthage* and used it throughout the ground floor, creating a seamless flow from room to room.

the whole family,' says Bénédicte. 'Alexandre completely understood.' The Petits also required enough bedrooms to accommodate their family comfortably, and reception rooms big enough for them to gather in. And, of course, they wanted to make the best of the spectacular views. As for aesthetics, they liked the idea of a house that looked as though it had stood here for centuries, but that also incorporated the best of 21st-century living – air conditioning, a cinema room, a swimming pool, an efficient modern kitchen with space for informal entertaining, and plenty of storage.

Alexandre Lafourcade has given them all these things and more. Working within the footprint of the farm buildings, he has created a house that looks a good 300 years old from the outside, its long facade limewashed the colour of pale honey and pierced by windows with

gently arched tops flanked by wooden shutters painted dove grey. The front door is weathered in its surround of old stone, and the steps that lead up to it look as though they have been trodden by generations of prosperous farmers. It's a clever illusion. All that remains of the original buildings is their outline, and the positioning of a few windows. Most of the windows are new, and the front door may be weathered, but not by time and use.

Once inside, the feel is contemporary, with smooth stone floors in shades of grey, and minimal detailing. The entrance hall leads to

LEFT The kitchen is at the opposite end of the house from the living room, and is recessed under the upper terrace such that its doors open onto a broad, shaded area where there is a table at one end and armchairs and a sofa at the other, doubling the available space all through the summer when life is lived outdoors. The house is extremely well equipped but nothing need be on show thanks to the well-designed and generous storage. In separate rooms behind the kitchen, floor-to-ceiling cupboards hold tableware, table linen, and a choice of glassware, plus a laundry room and a larder.

ABOVE OPPOSITE The dining room also has French doors that open onto the terrace outside the kitchen. Suitable for more formal entertaining, this is a room rarely used during the summer months.

ABOVE AND RIGHT In a house where shades of grey and neutral tones dominate, the bright pink of a linen tablecloth stands out in bold relief. The terrace is paved in the same grey stone that has been used indoors. Shutters and French windows stand open from the dining room, and there is a view through to the staircase hall, and to the library and living room beyond.

'We wanted a house that would be relaxing, serene, and a haven for the whole family,' says Bénédicte.

LEFT Every bedroom in this generously appointed house has its attendant bathroom, all with floors in the same *pierre de carthage* as has been used downstairs. While the exterior looks 18th century, the interior benefits from the inclusion of every possible contemporary convenience, from state-of-the-art plumbing and underfloor heating, to the simple luxury of fine-mesh fly screens that are integrated into every window frame and a necessary precaution against mosquitoes.

OPPOSITE ABOVE LEFT All the rooms are generously proportioned, as are communal spaces such as the staircase hall and the landing, giving the house a sense of expansive calm. At the foot of the staircase, a pair of double French doors opens onto the south-facing terrace at the back of the house.

OPPOSITE ABOVE RIGHT The straight lines of the bedside table, the radiator cover, the glass plinth, and the abstract painting create a pleasing geometry in the main bedroom. The bed is from Poliform and the painting is by Clément Simonnet.

OPPOSITE BELOW All the bedrooms are decorated with similar restraint in plain, neutral colours, and each is furnished with a double bed, a chair, bedside tables, and a desk.

a staircase hall and a stretch of reception rooms: the living room that occupies the western end, a billiard room next to it, and on the opposite side of the hall, a dining room, and beyond that, the kitchen. Upstairs are seven bedrooms, each with attendant bathroom. The eastern end of the upper floor is devoted to a suite of rooms that includes the main bedroom and bathroom, a dressing room, and an office. Bedroom, office, and hall open onto a balcony with its own seating and dining areas, and that creates beneath it a shaded verandah outside the kitchen.

Bénédicte asked her friend, garden designer May de Lasteyrie, to create a setting that would flow naturally into the surrounding landscape. The single, veteran plane tree behind the house was joined by two companions nearly as tall. These now provide pools of shade in the smoothly raked gravel of the broad terrace that runs along the south-facing back of the house. It is here that family and visiting friends live when the weather is hot – eating meals outside, under the shelter of the first-floor balcony, or beneath the four mulberry trees that

have been trained to make a dense umbrella of leaves. Wisteria wraps the stone pillars of the verandah and there are flowering laurels in giant planters placed between the windows. Opposite the house, two borders extend along the edge of the gravel, providing a foreground of rippling grasses rising on either side of wide steps up to the pool.

Like the interior, this is a garden with no fuss or frills, consisting instead of big gestures and grand vistas. Like the interior, it has a clutter-free, Zen-like calm – '*simple et sauvage*', as Bénédicte describes it. Even though it is a house with an acreage of floor space, Bénédicte says that, thanks to a layout that places their own suite of rooms directly above the hospitable kitchen, they feel as comfortable when there are just two of them as they do when there are 22. Sometimes in the summer, they organize big dinners and hire an orchestra for entertainment. They go walking in the Alpilles, they play tennis, they swim in the pool, they cook, watch films, play billiards. So much for the 'small property that did not require too much work'.

CULTIVATING
BEAUTY

There is no direct translation for the French word chartreuse. The closest equivalent is hunting lodge, or possibly dower house. But a chartreuse was not designed specifically for country sports, nor to accommodate the widow of an estate owner. Most date from the 17th and 18th centuries, and were built by noble families as small, rural retreats – places for quiet contemplation, and intimate, informal dinners – comfortable, unassuming, charming, and not in any way ostentatious. And if this sounds like a blueprint for the ideal country house in the 21st century, in the case of this particular chartreuse, it is.

PREVIOUS PAGES The front facade, which overlooks lawns and a long vista towards the music pavilion, is very nearly symmetrical. Central doors open on either side of the house, allowing a view through from the box parterre to the entrance courtyard, just as the two reception rooms that flank the hall have opposing windows in an arrangement known as *en lanterne*.

ABOVE AND OPPOSITE BELOW LEFT Hugging the house on this side is a formal box parterre, punctuated with box topiary and planted with lavender and roses. The door onto the parterre is framed by blue shutters, and has pretty wrought-iron railings.

OPPOSITE ABOVE The house presents different faces from different angles. From this side, Bernard says it looks more like a farm, where the kitchen door on the right opens onto the entrance courtyard. Bernard installed the early-18th-century dormer windows in the roof in order to convert the attic space into extra bedrooms. The shell motif shows that they originate from a house on the pilgrim route to Santiago de Compostela, the shell being the emblem used by pilgrims.

OPPOSITE BELOW RIGHT The view from an upstairs window of the parterre to one side of the entrance courtyard with a three-tier pleached hedge of clipped hornbeam behind it.

OPPOSITE The *grand salon* is the largest of the ground-floor reception rooms and occupies the corner of the house at the other end from the kitchen. The room is furnished with chairs from the 18th century, and a 17th-century chaise longue, the end of which can just be seen in this photograph. Above the carved stone chimney piece, a fragment of panelling acts as a pinboard for a changing selection of postcards and engravings. The 'silent companions' are nicknamed Fanny and Alexander.

ABOVE LEFT Pots of porcelain hollyhocks stand on a table in the central hall beneath a chandelier still wreathed with Christmas foliage, now dried to the colour of straw.

ABOVE RIGHT The rooms are *en enfilade*, giving a view from one end to the other – in this instance from the entrance hall, through the dining room, to the kitchen.

OVERLEAF Bernard considers the dining room to be the heart of the house, the focus of hospitality, and to that extent the most important room. Here the table has been extended to accommodate lunch for six.

Surrounded by 90 acres of Perigord meadow and woodland, and framed by a garden that contrasts clipped topiary and pleached hornbeams with clouds of scented roses and blousy peonies, this is a house of golden stone, its long, steeply pitched roof punctuated by three square towers and pierced by dormer windows. It is L-shaped and, according to its devoted owner Bernard Hautefort, presents different personalities depending on which side you are seeing it from. Inside the crook of the L, he says, it looks like a farmhouse. Go through the central door and out to the other side, turn back to gaze on the long facade, and it has 'a feel of *Le Grand Meaulnes*'. Go round to where the shorter leg of the L has a view across the flower gardens, and the building has 'a touch of Mozart'.

This is a house that Bernard wanted to own from the age of 15. Brought up in a town nearby – his mother, now in her nineties, still lives there – he used to come here for riding lessons. 'The house was owned by an English lady who bred Connemara horses,' he says. 'She was marvellous, wearing tweed always, with a big brooch, and a silk head-scarf tied under her chin.' When the house first came up for sale, and Bernard was at the beginning of the long career in investment banking that earned him the *Legion d'Honneur*, he tried to persuade his father to buy it. Later, while he was based in London, it came up for sale again and he bought it for himself, his wife, and his teenage son, as somewhere to come home to in a peripatetic existence that included stints in Tokyo, New York, and Sydney.

'The first thing we did was to lay out and plant a new garden,' he says. Thirty years on, the design has matured, as gardens do, and the garden has spread and been embellished; today there is also a music pavilion, a glass house, and a potager arranged around a second pavilion where he plans to hang a recently purchased portrait of Lady Hamilton alongside 18th-century engravings of lemons and lemon trees. The garden was a priority, as it continues to be, and when it came to the interior of the house, the aim was to make house and garden feel as closely interlinked as possible.

This ambition was well served by the layout, which, in its original 17th-century form, was a single-storey *enfilade* of rooms, each one spanning the width of the house. This simple arrangement had been tampered with by later generations, with the addition of partition walls. Once these had been removed, the flow, or fluidity, as Bernard calls it, was restored with a kitchen at the far end of the longest leg of the L, leading into a dining room, then an entrance hall, a *petit salon*, and at the far end the *grand salon*. Each of these rooms has windows on two sides and, in the case of all but the *grand salon*, they are opposite one another in an arrangement called *en lanterne*.

ABOVE The wall of the dining room opposite the fireplace is filled with cupboards, stacked with china and glass, offering a glorious choice of table settings.

RIGHT On a battered old side table in a window of the dining room stands an antique crib figure named 'Papageno' by Bernard's grandchildren. The large china cabbage next to it is a tureen.

FAR RIGHT Laid on a cotton printed tablecloth from India, the table setting for lunch combines hand-made pottery with Wedgwood plates that reproduce the 'Frog' dinner service commissioned by Catherine the Great in 1773.

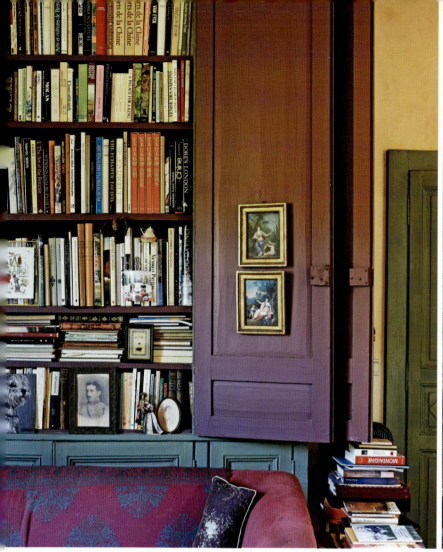

PAGE 173 Next to the dining room is the kitchen, its ceiling beams hung with old baskets, which Bernard uses for collecting fruit and vegetables from his abundant potager, or gathering flowers for the arrangements that decorate every room. The door to the dining room stands open.

OPPOSITE The *petit salon* is across the central hall from the dining room and mirrors its design, with windows lined up on opposite walls, *en lanterne*. In this room, the dominant colours are rich shades of plum in a variety of upholstery fabrics, from the Rubelli damask on the armless chairs, to the Indian cotton bought in a Mali market on the sofa, and also picked up in the striped fabric by Le Manach.

ABOVE A cupboard opposite the fireplace, painted dark sea green on the outside and aubergine/ eggplant on the inside, is crammed with a tiny proportion of Bernard's collection of books.

ABOVE RIGHT Among the antiques, the fine china, the paintings and engravings, are many playful pieces. Here on a desk in the corner, a pot in the shape of a long-horned ram, two turbaned candle bearers, and a cut-out cardboard elephant with a dog balancing on his back.

RIGHT Propped on the mantelpiece are two 17th-century paintings of flowers, picked up by Bernard for a few euros from the French equivalent of a junk shop.

RIGHT When this house was built, the space under its roof would have been used for storage. However, the height and steep pitch of the timbers mean there is plenty of space, and Bernard has converted the whole attic into a series of charming rooms by adding dormer windows. This is the biggest of the rooms, and is a library and office, with triangular windows on two sides set between the beams.

BELOW Despite the abundance of bookshelves in the house, books spill out into piles on chairs, occasional tables, sofas, and daybeds.

'When the windows on both sides are open,' says Bernard, 'goldfinches fly through from the front garden to the back.' In planning the garden, Bernard has always taken care to create vistas from the inside looking out. There are no curtains to intervene, just the gentle distortions of glass, much of which is 18th century. The external shutters can be closed against sunlight or the battering of storms. In the shorter leg of the L there is a guest bedroom and bathroom, and a corridor that takes you to Bernard's bathroom and his double-height bedroom, where there are windows on three sides.

Bernard's choice of materials, and of colours, intensifies the dialogue between the natural world outside and the domestic world within. Floors are reclaimed clay tiles, or oak boards. The staircase is carved from elm and all the ceilings are lined with lime tree planks, as is traditional in this part of France.

OPPOSITE This is the roof space above the *grand salon* at one end of the house. Bernard's desk sits in front of bookshelves made around sections of antique panelling, and is back-lit by sunlight pouring through a small oval window at floor level. Some of the pegs that pin the rafters can be seen protruding like spiky wooden stalactites.

ABOVE LEFT Bernard created these attic bedrooms for his grandchildren, Clémence and Antonin, who spent much of their childhood with him, enjoying the countryside he knows so well and loves so dearly. An antique bed fits neatly under the rafters.

LEFT The fragment of elaborate carving on the mantelpiece in Bernard's bedroom was a present to him from the antiques dealers who supplied much of the architectural salvage, including carved stone window frames, chimney pieces, and panelling, with which he restored the house. The angel's face has been sawn off, probably by the anti-religious revolutionaries who targeted churches during the French Revolution. The fireplace, not seen in the other photographs of this bedroom, is to the left of the windows one above the other opposite the bed.

ABOVE AND OPPOSITE Bernard's bedroom is a double-height space at the far end of the shorter wing of the house, its ceiling soaring high above the imposing half-tester bed. There are windows on three sides and no curtains. Bernard has never had, nor wanted, curtains, preferring there to be no fabric hindering the view of his surrounding gardens, a view he has taken care to cultivate from every angle. Most of the antique furnishings in the house are painted, but in this room, pieces from the 17th and early 18th centuries are dark, polished wood, giving the room a more masculine feel.

'I have collected many things over the years,' says Bernard, 'so that this house is a summary of my life, its contents like the feathers of my nest.'

Walls have the texture of stone, thanks to lime plaster, and colours are the soft hues of ripe summer fruit – plum, apricot, cantaloupe melon – the dusty green of sage leaves, the warm grey of weathered oak.

Two years after buying the house, Bernard suffered the tragic loss of his wife. Work on the house slowed and then stalled. It began again in earnest when his son had children, a boy and a girl, and Bernard converted the tall, beamed triangle of roof space to make bedrooms for them, adding dormer windows and a staircase, and making himself a library with shelving that reaches up into the rafters. Antonin and Clémence are now young adults, still Bernard's pride and joy, and still visiting this house full of books and music where they spent so much of their childhood.

Sprinkled among the elegant furnishings, which range in period from 17th century to Directoire, are things that must have amused them greatly as children. There is a table bustling with a flock of china tureens in the shape of birds. There is a beautifully modelled crib figure carrying a birdcage in one hand and a basket of fruit in the other, whom they

OPPOSITE In Bernard's bathroom, next to his bedroom, the ceiling height drops, as there is a bedroom and bathroom in the attic space above. While there are old floorboards in the bedroom, here there are reclaimed terracotta tiles. The walls are panelled to dado level and painted in rich shades of dark blue and plum. The chair is a *chauffeuse*, so called because of its low seat, designed to be pulled close to an open fire to make the most of its warmth.

LEFT In this attic bathroom, a high-backed country chair with a rush seat stands next to the antique tub.

ABOVE This ground-floor guest bedroom is in the wing of the house that also contains Bernard's bedroom and bathroom. Its bathroom has the original shaped, wooden bed alcove, now filled by a roll-top bathtub. The cupboard on the left houses a shower, and the one on the right, the lavatory. The painted wooden chair with a carved shell motif is 18th century Swedish, and the potted tulips on the bedside table are porcelain.

named 'Papageno'. Wooden tulips are lined up along the mantelpiece of the *grand salon*, and a couple of toy snails creep along the ceiling beams in one of the attic bedrooms. Then there are 'Fanny' and 'Alexander', silent companions painted on board, life-size portraits of children wearing small versions of the late-17th-century fashions of their elders. 'I have collected many things over the years,' says Bernard, 'so that this house is a summary of my life, its contents like the feathers of my nest.'

ABOVE AND ABOVE RIGHT Bernard continues to work on the garden, adding buildings as well as plants. He built this 'music pavilion' in honour of his granddaughter, Clémence. Although a new building, it has a patina of age thanks to the use of antique elements such as the doors and fanlight, and inside, the floor tiles and chimney piece.

OPPOSITE AND RIGHT Bernard placed an old engraving behind the foxed glass of the antique mirror. The roses in black Wedgwood vases are echoed by the porcelain flowers of the chandelier, each one a present from a guest at Bernard's 70th birthday celebrations.

It is difficult to imagine interior decorator Catherine-Hélène Frei von Auffenberg, or her German husband, author Pierre Frei von Auffenberg, living in a caravan. Not even a caravan with a chandelier and candles. Would Catherine still wear white linen and dangly earrings? Would Pierre's immaculate suit and handsome moustache survive? Sixteen years ago, their home for two months was, in Catherine's words, 'a very small caravan' in the garden of their recently purchased 13th-century castle in the village of Pampelonne in southwest France. 'Initially, Pierre said he would not be able to live in the caravan for more than a week, despite the chandelier I had installed for him,' says Catherine. 'But it had to be longer. The house was uninhabitable. Every night we went to a local farmer for a shower.'

PREVIOUS PAGES Built as a military stronghold in the late 13th century, this handsome castle has gradually been domesticated over the centuries. Today only one of its towers survives, its thick walls have been pierced by windows, and there is pavement and a tarmac road where once there would have been a moat.

ABOVE LEFT When the house was divided, this staircase that sweeps across the back wall of the entrance hall was created. It rises from a floor of new stone tiles that Catherine distressed using a mixture of acid and lime.

ABOVE AND OPPOSITE Next to the kitchen there is a cosy winter sitting room with a window at the front onto the street, and a window at the side that overlooks the garden. A pair of stone hounds guard the door to the entrance hall, one of which can be seen here. On the other side of the entrance hall, the door to the dining room stands open.

Catherine is glamorous, but she is also practical and enjoys getting her hands dirty on a building project. Over a long career as an interior decorator – a talent she discovered when she first met Pierre 40 years ago, aged 18, and decided to redecorate his house in Chelsea – she has laid floors, plastered walls, and generally mucked in with the builders and artisans who work with her. 'Pierre was older than me, well established, and editor of a German weekly called *Quick* when I first knew him,' she says. 'We loved London, but craved the solitude and peace of the countryside. We found a farmhouse in Wales where Pierre could escape to concentrate on writing, and I could learn how to restore an old building.' Here she also met her mentor, Monica Rawlins, artist, aristocrat, and friend of Augustus John. 'Monica was a very old lady, but still wonderfully stylish. She took me under her wing and encouraged me enormously.'

After 20 years in London and Wales, they decided to return to France. Back on home ground, as well as working for clients, Catherine undertook a series of house restorations for their own use, including a shepherd's smallholding in the Pyrenees, and a townhouse on the banks of the River Tarn. Looking for more space and a garden, in 2000 they viewed a property that dated from 1285, a castle that had once formed the centre of a fortified town known in this part of France as a *bastide*. 'It belonged to a retired colonel who was using it as a retreat from frequent rows with his wife. He only occupied a couple of rooms,' says Catherine. 'There were 600 empty whisky bottles in the old coach house.'

OVERLEAF On the first floor, at the front of the house, is this elegant *salon*. The Empire fireplace, the cornicing, and the panelled doors were intact, but the floor was covered in a layer of concrete. Catherine painstakingly chipped it off to reveal a parquet of unusual beauty, its variegated hardwoods radiating from a central star motif. The door to the left of the fireplace leads into Catherine's study and dressing room.

OPPOSITE AND BELOW When they bought the house, the kitchen had been divided into three separate rooms. Catherine restored its proportions and installed a range cooker in the huge fireplace opposite the sink. The only storage in this room is the open shelving under the work surfaces, leaving walls free from cupboards. This is possible because through the door into the winter living room, on the right, there is a door into the tower, a space that Catherine uses as a pantry and larder.

RIGHT Catherine made the kitchen work surface by burnishing powdered concrete with ice wrapped in a towel.

The spiral staircase inside the tower had collapsed, the shutters were hanging off their hinges and permanently closed, rooms had been clumsily partitioned and ceilings lowered, clay floor tiles had been painted gloss red and yellow, and there was only the most rudimentary wiring and plumbing. However, Catherine promptly decided they should buy it, partly because they were both entranced by the Sleeping Beauty romance of a castle with a tower and a garden completely overgrown with brambles, partly because the price reflected its ruinous state. Not many people would have been brave enough. 'Friends thought we were absolutely mad. They said it would be a disaster. But they changed their minds when they came back a year later.'

A year is how long it took to do the essential work of clearing and demolition that allowed them to see the full potential of this building. Many original features survived, including all

OPPOSITE It is hard to believe that the dining room was being used as stabling when Catherine and Pierre bought the house. It still retains rustic wooden beams, but has been comprehensively glamorized with lavish brocade curtains, which pull across a pair of reclaimed French doors, and the sparkle of antique glass and a crystal chandelier. Just visible through the doors is the old coach house.

ABOVE The first-floor rooms on either side of the blue salon are Pierre and Catherine's respective studies, the former lined with bookshelves and painted dark green. Catherine's study has a desk between its two windows, but is as much dressing room as office, centred on a daybed, piled with scarves and handbags. As in the salon next door, the floor is parquet, but here in a herringbone design.

RIGHT AND FAR RIGHT The portrait above the sideboard in the dining room is of an 18th-century Mexican courtesan, whose sidelong glance is splendidly suggestive. Above the stone chimney piece, which Catherine bought in pieces and restored, is a framed fragment of *toile de Jouy* wallpaper she found when redecorating the salon.

the chimney pieces, a beautifully simple sweep of staircase added when the building was divided to make two houses in the early 18th century, and wide floorboards as glossy as conkers on the second-floor landing. While the ground floor has a baronial feel, with its beamed ceilings and grand entrance hall, the first floor is neoclassical. The staircase runs across the back of the building, lit by windows overlooking the garden. On this floor on either side of the stairs are two bedrooms and adjoining bathrooms. Across the landing, at the front of the house, is a salon with long windows, a high ceiling, and its full complement of classical detailing, from a deep cornice, to pedimented architraves, panelled doors, and a parquet floor laid in bands of different hardwoods that radiate from a central star motif. It was hidden under a layer of concrete, which Catherine spent months chipping off on hands and knees.

BELOW Suspended from an antique, gilded pelmet, these lace curtains complete the romantic decor of this feminine bedroom. As in the other principal rooms on this level, the floor is polished parquet. There is a view over the back garden towards the 17th-century pavilion at its far end.

ABOVE AND OPPOSITE On the first floor there are two bedrooms at the back of the house on either side of the central staircase, both decorated in a late-18th-century style. The walls of this room are not panelled, but Catherine has created the effect of panelling by decorating with areas of wallpaper, and portraits of the period, which she has glazed and distressed, and framed with lines of paint. In the corner of the room, a door leads into the tower that once enclosed the staircase. This had collapsed when Catherine bought the house and she has converted the circular space to make bathrooms.

OVERLEAF Arriving on the top floor feels like travelling back in time at least a hundred years from the 18th-century interiors of the floor below, partly because it retains wide, early floorboards, partly because ceilings are lower under the fish-scale tiled mansard roof. Catherine has decorated the middle room as a boudoir, its chaise longue upholstered in *toile de Jouy*, its cupboard doors decorated with panels of antique wallpaper. A piece of antique *toile* is draped across the foot of the chaise longue, and the cushions are also covered in antique fabric.

'Friends thought we were absolutely mad. They said it would be a disaster. But they changed their minds when they came back a year later.'

ABOVE LEFT AND RIGHT The top-floor bathroom, once a bedroom, is furnished with a charming daybed with curving ends. The timber frame of the internal room partitions is a clue to the age of a building that has been through many changes and different incarnations over its 700-year history. The wooden frame of an old screen, hung with antique linen sheets, surrounds the shower.

OPPOSITE At the centre of this top-floor bedroom is a four-poster bed from IKEA that has been transformed by Catherine, with paint and a canopy of antique chintz. The cupboard to the left of the window, built into the thickness of the walls – one of the few remaining clues that this building was once a castle – has a door made from an old window.

The stripping out took a year, but it was another three years until the work was finished. 'My priority was to make a study for Pierre,' says Catherine, so this small room, lined with bookcases and leading off the first-floor salon, was the first room to be decorated. As work progressed, the cantilevered staircase, declared entirely safe by an engineer despite its disconcerting camber, was nonetheless given the added support of two steel pillars. The space to the right of the hall, which had been used as stabling, was converted to make a laundry room at the front, and a pretty dining room at the back where an 18th-century carved stone fireplace, bought in several pieces and restored by Catherine, contrasts with the rough, whitewashed beams. And the tower with its collapsed staircase became a larder and utility room on the ground floor, where the surviving lower steps make shelving for

groceries. On the two floors above, the space is used as bathrooms with walk-in showers enclosed within the curving stonework.

Every room displays Catherine's boundless creativity, ingenuity, and inventive use of materials. In the entrance hall she laid the floor herself, distressing the new stone tiles with acid and lime for a patina of age. The kitchen work surface, which has the silky finish of polished marble, was made by sprinkling powdered concrete and burnishing it with an ice pack wrapped in a towel. 'I love to experiment,' she says. 'You just need the confidence to try things out.'

Catherine's next personal project is a medieval townhouse. The castle is for sale and she is moving on. She has already started the process of transformation on this much smaller property, and found a way to make IKEA kitchen units look antique.

UK SOURCES

Every home owner, bar one, cited *brocantes* and *vides greniers* as the source for some of their furnishings. Many used local craftsmen to restore, adapt, and make furnishings and fittings for their homes. Such craftspeople and markets are best found locally, by word of mouth. Almost every owner also used elements of architectural salvage.

ARCHITECTURAL SALVAGE

English Salvage
North Road
Leominster
Herefordshire HR6 OAB
+44 (0)1568 616205
Architectural salvage including a particularly extensive selection of reclaimed French louvred shutters, flaking paint and all.

LASSCO
Brunswick House
30 Wandsworth Road
London SW8 2LG
+44 (0)20 7394 2100
Branches in Bermondsey and Oxfordshire.
www.lassco.co.uk
One of the first and still one of the best: a huge stock of everything from fireplaces to floors to stained glass, panelling and staircases.

Oak Beam UK
Ermin Farm
Cricklade Road
Cirencester
Gloucestershire GL7 5PN
+44 (0)285 869222
www.oakbeamuk.com
www.oldoakfloor.com
Old oak beams reclaimed and sourced in France. Also antique oak floor boards from France.

Norfolk Reclaim Ltd
Helhoughton Road
Hempton
Fakenham
Norfolk NR21 7DY
+44 (0)1328 864743
www.norfolkreclaim.co.uk
Reclaimed building materials including pantiles and pamments, plus architectural antiques and furnishings.

Walcot Reclamation
The Depot
Bath Road
Farmborough
Somerset BA2 0BD
+44 (0)1761 472074
www.walcotarchitecturalsalvage.co.uk
Traditional building materials and architectural antiques.

BATHROOMS

Antique Bathrooms of Ivybridge
Erme Bridge Works
Ermington Road
Ivybridge
Devon PL21 9DE
+44 (0)1752 698250
www.antiquebaths.com
Reconditioned antique baths plus reproduction ranges.

Balineum
www.balineum.co,uk
Online bathroom fittings and accessories and a range of pretty hand-painted tiles.

C P Hart
www.cphart.co.uk
Inspiring showrooms for kitchens as well as bathrooms.

Stiffkey Bathrooms
89 Upper St Giles Street
Norwich NR2 1AB
+44 (0)1603 627850
www.stiffkeybathrooms.com
Antique sanitaryware and their own range of period and bespoke bathroom accessories.

The Water Monopoly
10–14 Lonsdale Road
London NW6 6RD
+44 (0)20 7624 2636
www.watermonopoly.com
Opulent period bathtubs, basins, and fittings.

FABRICS

Bennison Fabrics
16 Holbein Place
London SW1W 8NL
+44 (0)20 7730 8076
www.bennisonfabrics.com
Chintzes, florals, stripes, and damasks in gentle colours.

Chelsea Textiles
13 Walton Street
London SW3 2HX
+44 (0)20 7584 5544
www.chelseatextiles.com
Gorgeous embroidered cottons, delicate prints, linens, silks, and voiles, many with a distinctly 18th-century feel.

Colefax and Fowler
110 Fulham Road
London SW3 6HU
+44 (0)20 7244 7427
www.colefax.com
Quintessentially English fabrics and wallpapers, but also excellent for checks, ginghams, and stripes.

GP & J Baker
Design Centre East
Chelsea Harbour Design Centre
London SW10 OXF
+44 (0)20 7351 7760
www.gpjbaker.co.uk
Comprehensive range of fabrics including both traditional and contemporary designs.

Ian Mankin
www.ianmankin.co.uk
Natural fabrics, including unbleached linens, butter muslin, and striped tickings.

Lewis & Wood
www.lewisandwood.co.uk
Large-scale fabrics and papers, including a fabric called Nantes that looks like an antique French quilt.

Pierre Frey
www.pierrefrey.com
Traditional French fabric and furnishing house producing many historic designs.

Russell & Chapple
30–31 Store Street
London WC1E 7QE
+44 (0)20 7836 7521
www.russellandchapple.co.uk
Artist's canvas, jutes, fine muslin, deckchair canvas and hessian sacking.

ANTIQUE FABRICS

Beyond France
+44 (0)1285 641867
www.beyondfrance.co.uk
Vintage linens, including monogrammed Hungarian grain and flour sacks and Romanian checked throws and tablecloths.

Katharine Pole
+44 (0)7747 616692
www.katharinepole.com
A wonderful selection of French antiques, particularly textiles.

Talent for Textiles
www.talentfortextiles.com
Antique textiles fairs throughout the West Country, bringing together dealers from all over the country.

FITTINGS

Brass Foundry Castings
www.brasscastings.co.uk
More than 800 brass and foundry castings reproduced from 17th- to 20th-century originals.

Clayton Munroe
www.claytonmunroe.com
Traditional handles and country style aged iron hinges and latches.

Jim Lawrence
www.jim-lawrence.co.uk
Ironwork with a hand-forged feel, from curtain poles and door handles to lighting and furniture.

FURNITURE – contemporary

The Conran Shop
81 Fulham Road
London SW3 6RD
+44 (0)20 7589 7401
www.conranshop.co.uk
Modern furniture and accessories that mix well with antiques and look good in older buildings.

Heal's
196 Tottenham Court Road
London W1T 7LQ
+44 (0)20 7636 1666
www.heals.co.uk
Good-quality contemporary furniture.

IKEA
www.ikea.com
Good design, piled high and sold cheap.

OKA
www.okadirect.com
Well-designed mid-price furnishings and accessories.

Poliform UK
276–278 King's Road
London SW3 5AW
+44 (0)20 7368 7600
www.poliformuk.com
Elegant modern furnishings, as used in the mas designed by Alexandre Lafourcade.

SCP
135–139 Curtain Road
London EC2A 3BX
+44 (0)20 7739 1869
www.scp.co.uk
Contemporary British designers,
including Matthew Hilton.

FURNITURE – antique, vintage and traditional

Alfies Antiques Market
13–25 Church Street
London NW8 8DT
+44 (0)20 7723 6066
www.alfiesantiques.com
Vintage, retro, and antique pieces.
A good source of mid-century modern.

Anton & K
Unit 5 Elms Farm
Gretton
Cheltenham
Glos GL54 5HQ
+44 (0)1242 602644
By appointment only.
www.antonandk.co.uk
French and Swedish decorative
antiques and painted furniture.

Bed Bazaar
The Old Station
Station Road
Framlingham
Suffolk IP13 9EE
+44 (0)1728 723756
www.bedbazaar.co.uk
Antique metal and wooden beds
and mattresses made to order.

The French House
The Warehouse
North Lane
Huntington
York YO32 9SU
+44 (0)1904 400561
www.thefrenchhouse.co.uk
All manner of French antiques,
from armoires to birdcages and baths.

French Loft
The Old Brewery
Fitzalan Road
Arundel BN18 9JP
+44 (0)1903 882725
www.frenchloft.com
Industrial, mid-century modern,
and European antiques.

George Smith
587–589 Kings Road
London SW6 2EH
+44 (0)20 7384 1004
www.georgesmith.com
Capacious and relaxed traditional
sofas and armchairs.

Joanna Booth Antiques
+44 (0)20 7352 8998 for an
appointment
www.joannabooth.co.uk
Early and rare antiques including
sculpture and tapestries.

Maison Artefact
273 Lillie Road
London SW6 7LL
+44 (0)20 7381 2500
www.maisonartefact.com
French and Swedish antiques
from the 18th to the 20th centuries,
including chandeliers and mercury
glass mirrors.

Simon Horn Furniture Ltd.
638–640 King's Road
London SW6 2DU
+44 (0)20 7731 3555
www.simonhorn.com
Classic French beds with caned
ends, and sleigh beds.

Talisman
79–91 New Kings Road
London SW6 4SQ
+44 (0)20 7731 4686
www.talismanlondon.com
Inspiring mix of unusual antiques.

FLOORING

Alternative Flooring Company
www.alternativeflooring.com
Coir, sea-grass, sisal, jute, and wool
floor coverings.

Bernard Dru Oak
www.oakfloor.co.uk
Specialists in oak flooring, most
of which is cut from the company's
own Exmoor woodlands.

Delabole Slate
www.delaboleslate.co.uk
Riven slate or slate slabs suitable for
work surfaces, fireplaces, and flooring.

Reclaimed Tile Company
www.reclaimedtilecompany.com
Antique French terracotta floor tiles
in all shapes and sizes.

Roger Oates
www.rogeroates.com
Natural floorings: chunky abaca,
plus flat-weave rugs and runners
in subtle stripes and felt matting.

Rush Matters
www.rushmatters.co.uk
Rush matting made with English
rushes; also baskets and rush
seating for chairs.

Victorian Woodworks
www.victorianwoodworks.co.uk
All types of reclaimed, new and
antique timber flooring and joinery.

HEATING

Bisque
244 Belsize Road
London NW6 4BT
+44 (0)20 7328 2225
www.bisque.co.uk
Suppliers of classic radiators.

Wharton Antiques
www.whartonantiques.com
Antique and reclaimed chimney
pieces from France.

The Windy Smithy
www.windysmithy.co.uk
Bespoke woodburning stoves
handcrafted in Devon.

FINISHING TOUCHES

Astier de Villatte
www.astierdevillatte.com
Handmade French ceramics available
from various stockists, including:
Liberty
www.liberty.co.uk
Bergdorf Goodman
www.bergdorfgoodman.com
ABC Carpet & Home
www.abchome.com

Graham & Green
www.grahamandgreen.co.uk
Glass, cushions, tableware, lighting,
and a small range of furniture
including leather.

KITCHENS

Fired Earth
www.firedearth.com
Kitchens (and bathrooms and tiles)
with a handcrafted feel, also an
excellent range of paint colours.

Plain English
www.plainenglishdesign.co.uk
Elegant, simple wooden kitchens
that are just as suitable for a French
country kitchen as an English one.

PAINT

Edward Bulmer
www.edwardbulmerpaint.co.uk
*Eco-friendly paints in a wonderful
selection of historic colours.*

Francesca's Paints
www.francescaspaint.com
*Traditional limewash, eco emulsion
paint, and chalky emulsion.*

The Little Greene Paint Company
www.thelittlegreene.com
A large range of colours.

Papers and Paints
www.papersandpaints.com
*In addition to their own excellent
range of paints, this company will
mix any colour to order.*

LIGHTING

John Cullen
561–563 Kings Road
London SW6 2EB
+44 (0)20 7371 5400
www.johncullenlighting.co.uk
*Contemporary light fittings and a
bespoke lighting design service.*

Vaughan
www.vaughandesigns.com
*Replica period lighting from lamps
to sconces to chandeliers.*

PLASTERWORK

Tom Verity
+44 (0)7932 752957
Recommended by Ursula Falconer.

WALLCOVERINGS

De Gournay
112 Old Church Street
London SW3 6EP
+44 (0)20 7352 9988
www.degournay.com
*Reproductions of hand-painted
18th-century Chinese wallpapers –
the sort of thing you might use
in a chateau.*

OUTDOORS

Cox and Cox
www.coxandcox.co.uk
*Online homewares, including
curly metal garden furniture with
a French feel.*

David Austin Roses
www.davidaustinroses.com
*Glorious English roses for gorgeous
French gardens – see Fiona Atkins
and Bernard Hautefort.*

Violet Grey
www.violetgrey.co.uk
*Antique and vintage garden
furnishings, some from France.*

US SOURCES

ARCHITECTURAL SALVAGE

Architectural Artifacts Inc.
architecturalartifacts.com
*Chicago-based architectural salvage
and unique antiques.*

Caravati's Inc.
104 East Second Street
Richmond, VA 23224
+1 804 232 4175
www.caravatis.com
*Restoration materials and
architectural details from old
buildings – clawfoot tubs, reclaimed
wooden shutters, and wooden flooring.*

BATHROOMS

The Bath Works
www.thebathworks.com
*Traditional-style tubs inspired
by antique and vintage cast-iron
examples, including copper and
brass slipper and soaking tubs.*

FABRICS

Rawganique
www.rawganique.com
*Unbleached and undyed French
linen sheets woven from organically
grown flax.*

Rough Linen
www.roughlinen.com
*Bedlinen and tablelinen with the
traditional texture and colour of
antique French linen.*

FITTINGS

Harrington Brass Works
+1 201 818 1300
www.harringtonbrassworks.com
*Traditional brass fixtures for kitchen
and home, especially faucets. Also
bathroom products.*

Marc Maison
www.marcmaison.com
*Specialists in authentic French
antique fireplace mantels. Also
overmantels and mirrors, doors,
and lighting.*

FURNITURE – antique, vintage and traditional

Beall & Bell
430 Main Street
Greenport, NY 11944
+1 631 477 8239
www.beallandbell.com
*American, French, and English
antiques and industrial pieces.*

Dovetail Antiques
252 Highway 107 South
Cashiers, NC 28717
+1 828 743 1800
www.dovetail-antiques.com
Importer of French antiques.

Dreamy Whites
www.dreamywhitesonline.com
*French antiques for an authentic
old French farmhouse feel.*

Joyce Horn Antiques
7065 Old Katy Road
Houston, TX 77024
+1 713 688 0507
www.joycehornantiques.com
*Fine European antiques and
reproduction furniture.*

Kim Faison Antiques
5605 Grove Avenue
Richmond, VA 23226
+1 804 282 3736
www.kimfaisonantiques.com
*Painted furniture from Scandinavia,
and France, and Delft.*

Red Chair Antiques
606 Warren Street
Hudson, NY 12534
+1 518 828 1158
www.redchair-antiques.com
*Antique furnishings and accessories,
many of them sourced in France.*

Restoration Hardware
www.restorationhardware.com
*Reproduction wooden sleigh beds,
French-style sofas, washed linen
sheets, 19th-century-style glass,
and metal chandeliers.*

HEATING

Chesneys
www.chesneys.com
*Modern and antique fireplaces,
including antique French designs.*

FLOORING

Exquisite Surfaces
www.xsurfaces.com
*Limestone flooring, European oak
floors, and both salvaged and newly
produced terracotta tiles. Also
antique and reproduction limestone
fireplaces. Showrooms nationwide.*

FINISHING TOUCHES

I Dream of France
www.idreamoffrance.com
*Provençal-style table linens from
France, as well as soaps and gifts.*

Madison and Muse
madisonandmuse.ca
*Pure linen bedding and table linens
and French flatware.*

PAINTS

Benjamin Moore
www.benjaminmoore.com
*The Colonial Williamsburg
collection contains historic colours
based on original pigments developed
more than 250 years ago.*

Old Village Paint
www.old-village.com
*Manufacturers of paint since 1816,
producing colour reproductions from
the Colonial, Federal, and Victorian
periods and stains and varnishes as
well as a special 'Couleurs de
Provence' collection.*

LIGHTING

House of Antique Hardware
www.houseofantiquehardware.com
*French-style chandeliers and wall
sconces and matching switch plates.*

OUTDOORS

Fermob
www.fermob.com
*Powder-coated metal benches, folding
tables and chairs. Manufacturers of
the classic Luxembourg low armchair,
as seen in the famous Paris park.*

French Garden House
www.frenchgardenhouse.com
*Antiques and decorative objects
for the house and garden.*

PICTURE CREDITS

Endpapers The home of Françoise Piccino, www.la-cabane-de-jeanne.com; 1 Irene Silvagni; 2–3 The home of Bert and Julia Huizenga, south of Toulouse at the foothills of the Pyrenees; 4 The Normandy home of Fiona Atkins of Town House, Spitalfields; 5 *above* Irene Silvagni; 5 *below right* The Normandy home of Fiona Atkins of Town House, Spitalfields; 6 The home of Sara Giunta and Jean-Luc Charrier of La Maison de Charrier in Valbonne; 7 The Normandy home of Fiona Atkins of Town House, Spitalfields; 8–9 The home of Françoise Piccino, www.la-cabane-de-jeanne.com; 10–23 The Normandy home of Fiona Atkins of Town House, Spitalfields; 24–37 The home of Françoise Piccino, www.la-cabane-de-jeanne.com; 38–47 The home of Ilse van der Meerakker owner of www.maisonvivreplus.nl; 48–63 Irene Silvagni; 64–73 The home of Nicole Albert, owner of House La France, which is available for rental at www.houselafrance.com; 74–89 The home of Bert and Julia Huizenga, south of Toulouse at the foothills of the Pyrenees; 90–105 Architecture in Miniature www.petergabrielse.com; 106–121 The home of Sara Giunta and Jean-Luc Charrier of La Maison de Charrier in Valbonne; 122–137 Thekla Benevello; 138–153 Michel Mulder and Sofie Sleumer, owners – creators – builders of *hôtel de campagne* D'une île, www.duneile.com; 154–163 A house in Provence designed by architect Alexandre Lafourcade, www.architecture-lafourcade.com; 184–201 Home of French interior designer Catherine-Hélène Frei, www.cathfrei.com; 205 Home of French interior designer Catherine-Hélène Frei, www.cathfrei.com.

BUSINESS CREDITS

Thekla Benevello
La Queurie
61150 La Courbe
France
T: +33 (0)2 33 12 85 68
E: thekla.benevello@gmail.com
www.laqueurie.wordpress.com
Pages 122–137.

D'une île
hotel – restaurant
Domaine de Launay
61110 Rémalard
France
T: + 33 (0)2 33 83 01 47
E: info@duneile.com
www.duneile.com
Pages 138–153.

Catherine-Hélène Frei
T: + 33 (0)6 87 34 79 52
Currently restoring another house; her chateau is for sale. Please visit www.cathfrei.com for details.
Pages 184–201, 205.

Peter Gabrielse
www.petergabrielse.com
Pages 90–105.

House La France
www.houselafrance.com
Pages 64–73.

Bruno Lafourcade
10 Boulevard Victor Hugo BP 75
13532 Saint-Rémy-de Provence
France

T: +33 (0)4 90 92 10 14
E: contact@architecture-lafourcade.com
www.architecture-lafourcade.com
Pages 154–163.

La Maison de Charrier
La Boutique La Maison de Charrier
1 rue Faubourg Saint Esprit
06560 Valbonne
France
T: +33 (0)4 93 40 29 19
Pages 6, 106–121.

Françoise Piccino
E: francoise.piccino@nordnet.co.uk
www.la-cabane-de-jeanne.com
Endpapers, pages 8–9, 24–37.

Irene Silvagni
Pages 1, 5 above, 48–63.

Town House
5 Fournier Street
Spitalfields
London E1 6QE
UK
www.townhousespitalfields.com
Pages 4, 5 below right, 7, 10–23.

Vivre+
Hoogstraat 38
3841BS Harderwijk
T: +31 (0)6 34 68 00 60
E: maison@vivreplus.nl
www.maisonvivreplus.nl
Pages 38–47.

ACKNOWLEDGMENTS

This is the sixth book I have written in partnership with Jan Baldwin,
a collaboration that has become one of the great pleasures of my working
life. Jan takes fabulous photographs and is faultlessly professional,
but she is also the best company. Photographic assistants Peter Dixon and
Shivantha Kanagaratnam were invaluable. I am equally fortunate to work
with a team of people at Ryland Peters & Small, who are as supportive as
they are creative: Jess Walton, whose inspired research and organizational
skills are key to the success of the project, Annabel Morgan, who is as
efficient and talented an editor as she is unfailingly encouraging, and Toni
Kay, whose elegant designs determine the look of the finished product.
Art director Leslie Harrington, production manager Gordana Simakovic
and editorial director Julia Charles, are just as vital to the process.
As for publisher Cindy Richards, without her there would be no book,
particularly as in this instance its subject was her initial idea. All the
house owners we met were warm, welcoming, and generous to a fault,
and they all spoke English much better than I speak French.
I hope they will feel we have done justice to their hard work,
their ingenuity, and, above all, their sense of style.